You Can Trust The New Testament

Refuting Bible Critics

Gerald Charles Tilley, PhD.

You Can Trust The New Testament

Refuting Bible Critics

California Biblical University Press

P.O. Box 973

Tustin, California 92781

Table of Contents

Table of Contents (cont.)

Appendices

Preface

This title grew out of a dream I had in which my wife after listening to a program of alleged experts on the Bible said to me, *"They are learning a lot of new information about the Bible."* In the dream I replied, *"No, they are just repeating many of the criticisms made over the last few centuries about the Bible and pretending that these ideas are new and that they have been proven true."* I then woke up, got up and began to write this preface.

I have been studying the Bible and attempts to discredit it since 1960. I have found that by far, most criticisms of the Bible are easily refuted. There are also some attacks that require more specialized knowledge to order to refute them. Areas in which special knowledge is sometimes needed includes that of the Hebrew, Aramaic, or Greek grammar; cultural practices of the first century; awareness of other ancient writings; and specific historical events or archaeological excavations.

The purpose of this publication is to provide evidence that supports the credibility and reliability of the New Testament portion of the Bible. In that process many of the skeptical attacks on the New Testament will be exposed as without rational support and useless. For the refuting of criticisms and falsely alleged contradictions of the Hebrew Scriptures, designated The Old Testament, see my earlier publications, <u>You Can Trust the Old Testament</u> and <u>Refuting Criticism and Alleged Contradictions of the Old Testament</u>.

Several appendices are added to this current volume to deal with some specific claims of skeptics or distortions of New Testament teachings. Unless otherwise indicated, all references from the Bible will be from the New American Standard Version or the New International Version.

The Old Testament, though superseded by the New Testament for the Christian faith is still of great significance for Christianity. Without the Old Testament we would lack information regarding origins, New Testament fulfilments of prophecy would be meaningless as would hundreds of references in the New Testament to otherwise unknown people and events, promises of God, etc. It is my hope and intention that in addition to believers being strengthened in their faith some non-believers are brought to faith through the evidence presented in this volume.

Introduction

This book is produced as an intended companion to an earlier work titled, <u>You Can Trust the Old Testament</u>. The other book was written first with no awareness that this companion might also be produced. It made sense, however, for the book on the Old Testament to be written first. Writing on the Old Testament first was like establishing the foundation for this present publication. This is because, although the New Testament is more authoritative, relevant, and significant for the Christian faith, without the Old Testament much of the New would not make sense nor be fully understood.

Without the Old Testament, we would be lacking vital information about the infinite personal God. We would be missing information on the origin of the universe, the origin of life, the origin of sin, and the origin of the promises of God to deal with and resolve the issues of human existence. We would also be missing the predictions regarding the promised Messiah that announce His coming and that enable us to identify Him from the many false messiahs. So, the effort and intention to demonstrate that the Old Testament was reliable and necessary preceded this present volume.

Now, however, it is time to do the same work to validate the authenticity, reliability, and relevance of the New Testament. It is important to validate the New Testament in order to separate it from the merely human musings, assumptions, intuitions, opinions, and assertions called world religions. These world religions have arisen throughout history as humanity turned away from the original knowledge of the true God (see my book <u>The Origin of Religion</u>). Humans generally have sought to diminish the Christian faith by including it among the world religions but it does not fit there.

My earlier publication, <u>The Uniqueness of the Christian Faith</u> demonstrates that the first century Biblical Christian faith is in a different category from those world religions. The Christian Faith is the restoration of the truth about God and man. The New Testament is presented as the final written truth God has chosen to reveal about Himself, man, and God's plan of redemption. It also presents as much as God has chosen to inform us regarding the future.

The infinite–personal God who created the universe and every living thing is so far beyond our finite minds that we could not know anything about Him except what we can deduce through creation unless He were to give us information about Himself. That is what is called special revelation and what the Old and New Testaments purport to be.

Most criticisms of the Bible are not new nor are they true. Most criticisms and objections to the reliability of the Bible been thoroughly refuted in the past by reason, logic, the science of textual criticism, history and/or archaeology. One method of dishonest or uninformed critics is to revive an old attack on the Bible that has previously been thoroughly discredited.

Once some time has passed and the vast majority of people have forgotten the argument and its resolution, it is presented again as if it were a new discovery or new insight that disproves the validity of the biblical scriptures or of the Christian faith. Since most people seem to have little or no awareness of the past and don't read old books, they can readily be deceived. An additional problem is that many who read the extravagant and widely publicized attacks on the Bible never read the answer or refutation of those attacks.

Most critics do not read writings that have exposed errors in their arguments and assertions or that present evidence in support of the Biblical Scriptures. Those who have read the evidence in support of the reliability of the biblical Scriptures seldom are able to lay aside their preconceived ideas and presuppositions. These world-view assumptions cause an inability or unwillingness to admit the strength, credibility, and significance of the evidence they are faced with. Therefore, the evidence contrary to their views does not affect their thinking. They are thus usually prevented from comprehending the fallacies in their beliefs.

When I write of refuting Bible critics, I am not referring to those who are involved in genuine textual criticism and historical research in order to determine the authentic and accurate text of the biblical Scriptures.

The critics I am referring to are those who write for popular media or scholarly journals whose anti-biblical, anti-supernatural biases control their declarations. Many of these negative critics are involved in so called 'Higher Criticism', 'Form Criticism' or 'the Jesus Seminar.' These are efforts intended to discredit and destroy confidence in the authenticity and credibility of the Bible. These critics use a variety of strategies to give their assertions and speculations the appearance of legitimate scholarship. Exposing these fraudulent assertions, false assumptions and unreliable conclusion are the focus of this publication.

There is one type of skeptical argument for which it is difficult to give satisfactory answers. That type of argument is the practice some opponents of the Christian faith have of making broad sweeping assertions instead of specific claims. An example is the oft repeated declaration, "The Bible is full of contradictions." Another unjustifiable assertion is that "The history presented in the Bible is unreliable." It can be honestly replied that such assertions are false and misleading.

However, neither the false accusation nor the answer has proven anything. The skeptic is relying upon his or her position or reputation rather than upon valid argument or evidence. Unfortunately, such false statements attacking the Bible are often accepted as valid criticism by the uninformed public.

Some skeptics only use this type of assertion, because of the difficulty of refuting such general attacks. When the opponent gets to specific statements in the Bible, they are on less solid footing because specific information can be answered and explained.

In 1998, Kenneth C. Davis published Don't Know Much About The Bible. What he meant is that the rest of us didn't know much about the Bible and he was going to enlighten us. He lists a few examples of information about the Bible and Jesus that most people know to be true. He then proceeds to espouse skeptical assertions and assumptions as if they are of the same certainty as the previous facts, which they are not. He promotes a needlessly skeptical and negatively critical attitude toward the Biblical Scriptures. He begins his section on the New Testament by questioning what could we possibly know for certain about Jesus.

"How, then, can anyone get a 'true' picture of the 'historical' Jesus, a man who left no writings or Oval Office tape recordings? We are not even sure if the people who said they knew him really knew him or where they got their stories if they didn't." [1]

Though Jesus never wrote a book, he has stimulated the writing of thousands, including over two dozen by His closest original associates and followers. Reading the biblical Gospels by those not predisposed to skepticism presents a sense that these writers knew their subject very well.

There is no legitimate reason to deny their intimate relationship and knowledge of Jesus (Matthew, John, Peter, and James) and with those who gained knowledge from Jesus' family and associates (Mark and Luke). It is important to remember that anything can be asserted and inferred, but it must be determined how those speculations and opinions relate to the information to which we actually have access!

Davis goes on to say that, *"Apart from a smattering of references to Jesus in Roman-era writings, everything we commonly know about the man people called the 'Christ,' 'Messiah, and 'anointed one' comes from the New Testament, on the hearsay evidence of people who had an unshakable faith that this man was also the Son of God who died for their sins and then rose from the dead.*"[2]

First, it is important rather than dismissing that 'smattering of references' from the first and second centuries, to point out that they unintentionally confirm some important details in the Gospels relating to Jesus. This is especially significant in that those writers were not supportive nor sympathetic to the Christian faith. See some of those very early accounts in Appendix A. Secondly, information from those involved and from eyewitness testimony is the basis of most knowledge of the past. If Davis's attitude were applied to the rest of history, we would know virtually nothing for sure about the past.

It is also important to ask upon what basis did these people gain *"an unshakable faith*? They would not have assumed that this man was also the Son of God who would die for their sins and then rise from the dead merely because He said so. When one actually reads the documents, you find that the unshakable faith developed over time as Jesus proved to be the promised Messiah by His life and deeds that fulfilled his words as well as the words of much earlier prophets. Their unshakable faith was solidified following his forty days with them after his execution and resurrection. For a summary of the evidence confirming Jesus resurrection from the dead, see appendix D.

What is the New Testament?

The New Testament is the continuation and the renewal of revelation from God after a silence of about 450 years. There had been no prophet of God from the time of Malachi (c. 430 B.C.) until John the Baptist, (approximately 26 A.D.).

The New Testament is a collection of twenty-seven documents. The first four writings are memoirs of two of Jesus' original followers (Matthew & John); one written by a close associate of the apostle Peter and several other early followers of Jesus (Mark); and Luke, an associate of the apostle Paul. Luke's account resulted from personal research including interviews. Those writings are called the Gospels, meaning Good News.

The next writing, Acts, also by Luke, explains the birth of the Christian Church which resulted from the resurrection of Jesus and the coming of the Holy Spirit of God upon Jesus' apostles. It also presents some of the church's earliest history. Acts is followed by twenty letters from apostles and other first century Christian leaders. The final writing is a series of visions given to the apostle John regarding the churches and the future fulfillment of the plan and purposes of God.

It might be valuable to remember, as archaeologist John McRay reminds us, that for most of history, the Bible was not available as a complete text, bound with a table of contents, maps, and an index or concordance. During the early years of the church the individual writings circulated separately from the particular church or individual to whom that book had originally been sent."[3]

A little later, the Gospels began to be circulated together as did the letters of Paul. As churches became aware of new writings from these leaders, they eagerly sought to add to their collection. Gradually churches obtained more and more of the apostolic writings as they were copied and sent from the original receiving church to others.

Hindering this process of accumulating all the New Testament documents, in addition to the labor of hand copying each document and difficult communication, was the preference of hearing an apostle or other leader in person rather than merely reading what he had written. But as persecution flared up and some of these original leaders were killed, it became obvious that obtaining all of their writings was essential.

Soon heretical teachers began to travel around to the churches. Some of these frauds were claiming to be apostles. It became more and more important to have genuine apostolic teaching available to compare with what others were teaching and claiming. Then near the beginning of the second century (as well as later), fraudulent writings began to appear which claimed to be written by the apostles or other prominent church persons.

Even fraudulent 'sayings of Jesus' began to appear, like those in the so-called gospel of Thomas. Jesus had correctly informed the apostles that false prophets and false Christs would appear and these pretenders would deceive many (Matt. 24:4-11, 23-27).

Soon, men falsely claiming to be apostles, prophets, and evangelists appeared. The introduction of Gnostic and other apocryphal writings, combining truth with distortions and fiction, also were being presented as apostolic. This proved the necessity of having the apostle's teachings and traditions all in written form (which is the complete New Testament). It should be obvious that anything the apostles wanted us to know would have been written down by them or their closest associates.

Unfortunately, those perversions of the original teachings still occurred. One method of getting around the protection of the written apostolic teaching, has been to declare that these false teachings were the "*unwritten traditions of the apostles.*" Since unwritten traditions can be easily be created and/or altered, God would not leave His truth to be at the mercy of human invention and preferences. It was all written for us so we could have certainty as to what is from God.

A second method of altering the original apostolic teachings was the introduction of later writings falsely claiming to be from the apostles or other prominent people in the Gospels. These were rejected by the church but have become championed by some skeptical scholars as a means of discrediting the authentic Scriptures and the Christian faith.

There is also a third method of distorting the original apostolic faith, which is to claim that only the church (meaning the church hierarchy) can authentically interpret the scriptures. This claim resulted in scripture being interpreted in the light of, or by the growing body of human traditions and practices. In other words, human preferences became the authority instead of the scriptures. Instead of interpreting scripture by the traditions, the traditions should have been evaluated in the light of scripture. The process was reversed which eliminated the actual authority of scripture. This led to increasingly ignoring and dismissing the actual teachings of the scriptures.

Related to the above methods is another huge mistake which completed the process of altering the Christian faith into a mere religion. This error was the decision in 380 A.D. of Theodosius I to make Christianity the state religion of the Roman Empire. Constantine had issued the edict of toleration in 313 A.D. which legalized Christianity and made the state neutral in regards to religion. But in 380 A.D., suddenly everyone born in the empire was considered to be Christian. Previously only those who made a specific personal confession of faith were considered believers.

With the state securing and financially involved in supporting Christianity, church positions became a desirable and secure career. Many men who were perhaps 'Christianized', but not truly converted, sought, and obtained positions in the church. There were many who now used the church to gain wealth, prestige, and power. It was being changed into a religion that served the interests, desires, and goals of those in the system rather than a faith that transformed men's lives and societies.

A special clerical class developed who claimed to be in charge of the scriptures, the church, and the means of salvation. This enabled ambitious, self-seeking (and often unconverted) church leaders to withhold the scriptures from the common people. They could also threaten to withhold the means of salvation from those who opposed or disagreed with them. This contributed to the development of a complex church hierarchy and additional false teachings that distorted and even contradicted the biblical scriptures.

There have been many efforts throughout the centuries to restore the apostolic truth of biblical teaching to the church. Finally, movements in the direction of restoration and renewal succeeded in some countries during the fifteenth and sixteenth centuries.

The vast contrast between movements emphasizing biblical teaching and that of the Roman Catholic church became glaringly apparent to many throughout most of Europe.

Ultimately then, the New Testament is the complete collection of the authentic apostolic teachings. Anything not included in these documents was not intended by God to be accepted as genuinely inspired and apostolic. The New Testament is the legitimate standard, the measure by which all Church doctrine and all teaching is to be measured.

"Earlier opinions to the contrary not withstanding, these documents were probably written on codices rather than scrolls from the beginning ... the reason why Christians chose to use papyrus codices is not known, but may have been partially economical (the book form allowed writing on both sides of the sheet).The use of codices may also have been part of the ongoing religious and cultural separation between the Christian community and the Jewish community in the second century—a separation also seen in the church's use of the Greek translation of the Old Testament (the Septuagint) while the Jews used the Hebrew original, and the church's used the term ecclesia for their assemblies while the Jews used the term synagogue." [4]

Is Christianity the Only Complete Truth About God and Man?

Perhaps the first objection by skeptics that should be addressed is that of condemning Christians for claiming exclusivity to truth. That is the claim that the Christian faith is the only complete truth about God, as well as man, and that Jesus is the only way to God.

C.S. Lewis wrote *"But of course being a Christian does mean thinking that where Christianity differs from other religions, Christianity is right and they are wrong. As in arithmetic— there is only one right answer to a sum, and all other answers are wrong ..."* [5] This exclusivist claim of Christianity is routinely rejected and condemned as narrowminded and arrogant.

Instead, the evidence for the basis and reliability or unreliability of these claims should be objectively evaluated. This is usually avoided because most skeptics are not seeking an answer or the truth regarding this issue. They prefer to merely express their own opinions. Another fact the critics ignore is that virtually every religion claims to be the only true way.

> "No matter what belief system you adopt, you will be saying that your system is right and that the billions of people who don't accept it are wrong. If Islam is correct the billions of people who don't accept it are wrong. If orthodox Judaism is correct the billions of Gentiles are wrong. If it is correct to approve of multiple belief systems because they are all valid ways of achieving spiritual enlightenment, the billions of Christians, Jews and Muslims and others who believe in exclusive religions are intolerant and wrong."[6]

Rather than ignoring that most religions claim to have an exclusive knowledge of the truth, the intelligent and scholarly approach to such claims would be to examine and evaluate the credibility of those claims. Rather than merely assuming each religion has its own validity or that one is as valid as any other, the evidence in support of a truth claim needs to be assessed.

Are there truth claims that have a greater foundation in history and other aspects of reality that set it apart from most or all the others? There is a wide range of differences among the many possible answers available. Many of the truth claims made by a particular group or religion contradict the truth claims made by other groups. Logic affirms that they could all be wrong, but they cannot all be true. There are also methods of sorting out the reasonableness and validity of these various claims. C.S. Lewis wrote, *"There are a dozen views about everything until you know the answer. Then there is never more than one."*[7]

Part of the mistaken understanding in regard to religion is the false idea that all religions are essentially the same but vary as to superficial details. To believe that all religions are essentially the same, shows one has not honestly examined the various religions carefully in terms of their own claims. Once one does so, it becomes obvious that the minor details are sometimes similar, and it is the essentials that vary greatly.

Theologian Stanley Grenz wrote in this regard, that the religions do not all seek the same goal, they do not agree in their understanding of the human predicament nor as to the solution of it.[8] One of the other theologians who point out the shallow thinking of those who assert that all religions are essentially the same wrote,

> *"The commonalities among the various religions cannot obscure irreducible differences. A tendency to wish them away variously afflicts theologians, scholars of comparative religious studies, phenomenologists and religious activists alike. The differences among the world religions, which remain stubbornly irreconcilable, are the distinguishing characteristics of each religion ..."* [9]

It is not reasonable to merely accept all the contradictory claims as somehow all relevant and valid. Neither is it necessary to dismiss all the religions as ridiculous and false. Often the critic's presuppositions and bias blind them to reality and to differences among the religions. What would happen if they were to put aside their prior assumptions and really consider the evidence on its own merits?

Ravi Zacharias put it this way:

> *"All religions are not the same. All religions do not point to God. All religions do not say that all religions are the same. At the heart of every religion is an uncompromising commitment to a particular way of defining who God is or is not and accordingly, of defining life's purpose.*
>
> *"Anyone who claims that all religions are the same betrays not only an ignorance of all religions but also a caricatured view of even the best-known ones. Every religion at its core is exclusive."*[10]

It is significant to recognize that not all assertions are of equal value. Some are based upon actual eyewitness accounts and genuine evidence. Some assertions even have multiple eyewitnesses and confirming evidence. On the other hand, many assertions are merely the opinions, speculations or preferences of the individual declaring them. Obtaining group support or a consensus based upon such flimsy basis does not alter opinions into evidence. What then would be tests one could apply to sort out valid claims from mere assertions without validity?

One such test would be whether or not the claims of a religion or faith are founded upon genuine historical events and real people. Tied to that, would be the test of whether those historical references correspond to or contradict what is known about the history of those eras and cultures.

Another aspect of the historical test would be whether anachronisms exist within the religion or cult's alleged scriptures. Do those scriptures support mythologies or scientific errors that were believed at the time they were written. These prior tests alone would eliminate the validity of most religions and cults.

Another type of test would be that of consistency within the scriptures of that religion. Related to that would be the test as to whether the proclamations of the religion are found within their alleged scriptures. Some religious advocates espouse principles or ideas that have been picked up from another faith that has proven popular, though not an actual tenant of the adopting religion.

In addition, accepting the legitimacy of researching and evaluating the origin and sources of the religion's scriptures is important. Islam for example rejects the validity of such examination whereas Christianity welcomes it. Islam opposes such research because that would expose the falseness of Mohammad's claims to have received the Quran from the archangel Gabriel. A further test of authenticity would be, does the religion or faith give meaningful, realistic answers to the big questions.

Another test would be that of whether adherents of the religion can actually live as if the teachings correspond to reality. This would eliminate religions and philosophies for example that deny the reality of evil or of the material world such as Hinduism and the Christian Science religion.

It is important to realize that the claim that the Christian Faith is unique; that it is vastly different from the world religions, is not a claim that Christians have devised. The concept that Christianity is unique and the only complete truth about God are claims that originate in the Bible itself. In the Old Testament God said on many occasions that there was no other but Him "*I am the Lord, and there is no other; besides Me there is no God ...*" *Isaiah 45:5*. (See other examples of such statements in the Endnote.) [11]

In the New Testament it is clearly claimed by Jesus and the first believers that He was the only means of access to God the Father. Claiming Jesus is the only Savior and Lord is merely being true to what He taught us and to the evidence we see and experience. (*Matt. 1:21; John 8:24, 14:6; Acts 4:12; 1Tim. 2:5*).

Frequently Christians are asked why we say that Jesus is the only Savior. The answer requires a little background from the Old Testament. When the first humans sinned by disobeying God there were consequences of their action. The primary consequence was that of breaking the connection with God; a fundamental separation occurred between God and man. This was revealed in the man and woman's attempts to hide from God. That was the spiritual consequence.

There were other disconnections and consequences of that disobedience as well. These consequences included physical and psychological as well as relational disconnects between humans. As time has gone on these consequences have continued to become more severe.

God however, promised that He would provide the solution and resolution for all these things. Humans have found ways to cope and deal with the other consequences as well as substitutions for God's solution, but those methods do not restore a genuine relationship with the true God. Jesus is that God-provided solution to bring about reconciliation, the only genuine solution.

It is obvious that the claim that all religions teach essentially the same thing is untrue. It is also obvious religious claims that contradict each other cannot both be true. As in mathematics, not every answer is right or true. There is only one correct answer to an equation. The same is true in regard to spiritual reality. As mentioned earlier, C.S. Lewis wrote: "*There are a dozen views about everything until you know the answer. Then there is never more than one.*" [12]

There are many ways in which Christianity differs significantly from the world religions. Assertions that the uniqueness of Jesus and his claim to be God were later inventions of the church are handled in a later section of this presentation. Sufficient for the moment is the assertion that without the uniqueness of Jesus and his actual resurrection from the dead there would never have been such a thing as the New Testament church.

Can Christianity Be Proven True?

This question is frequently asked of believers during discussions relating to truth, faith, or religion. The answer depends upon what the questioner means by proven. If they mean can Christianity be proven true by the ordinary means of verifying past historical events, the answer is a definite yes. If they mean in the sense that science proves something through experimentation, or by measuring or analyzing elements or components, the answer is no.

A past event cannot be evaluated by the methods of science. Therefore, when someone claims that science has disproven (or proven) Christianity, the claim is bogus; completely fraudulent. But applying normal historical criteria can prove the events upon which the Christian faith is based are proven beyond a reasonable doubt.

Proof beyond a reasonable doubt is the basis of legal decisions. Waiting for 100% certainty would render most legal decisions impossible. In fact, most of daily life is based upon decisions made on the preponderance of evidence; probability not certainty. A high level of evidence is necessary but not 100% certainty. Paralysis would result if we were to require absolute proof for every important decision we face. Some people act as if absolute certainty is required before they will commit themselves to Christ.[13] This may just be a ruse to cover their unwillingness to embrace what they see as inconvenient truth.

Anyone willing to weigh and embrace the evidence regardless of where it leads, will come to know that Christianity is true. It is one of the most amazing aspects of Christianity, that its most astounding and incredible claims are anchored in the realm of ordinary human history. As apologist Josh McDowell wrote, *"The case for Christianity can be established by ordinary means of historical investigation."*[14]

History and Archaeological Evidence Regarding the Gospels

It is important to realize as retired professor John McRay wrote that *"We must also bear in mind that 'biblical archaeology' does not have reference to an independent discipline nor to a methodology peculiar to the Bible. Like classical archaeology, biblical archaeology exists not as a separate discipline, but as a field of inquiry within the general field of archaeology.*"[15]

The importance of this statement may not be obvious to some readers. McRay is indicating that the methods of excavating, discovering, classifying, dating, etc. that are utilized in biblical archaeology, are the same as those methods utilized in the general discipline of archaeology. This means it is not valid to ignore or dismiss discoveries made in biblical archaeology with the excuse that it is 'merely biblical archaeology.'

It is important to recognize what archaeology can and cannot do. Archaeology cannot prove the Scriptures to be the Word of God or of divine origin. What archaeology can do is confirm historical, geographical, cultural, and other details in the Scriptures. These confirmations add credibility to those documents, giving a basis for confidence that they are what they claim to be, revelation from the Creator.

There are, however, also skeptical scholars, often called minimalists, (or biblical deconstructionists) who seek to interpret evidence in such a way as to ignore or contradict its support of the scriptures. They often seek to undermine and minimize the relevance of discoveries that are supportive of the Scriptures. This bias against supernaturalism and the Bible are as pronounced and common within archaeology as within other fields.

The vast majority of people have no idea of the many hundreds of discoveries that confirm details in the Bible, which these skeptics have previously proclaimed as untrue. This is due both to the fact that most discoveries are only reported in academic journals and conference reports, and that the media seldom reports discoveries that demonstrate support for the validity of Scripture.[16] The purpose of this publication is to be one small corrective to these shortcomings.

Archaeology has proven to be a valuable discipline in the study and confirmation of the reliability of the New Testament, as it has of the Old Testament. This will no doubt continue to be true, as long as, and to the extent, that evidence is allowed to take precedence over speculations, theories, and preferences of scholars. However, as Jack

Lewis wrote *"In the New Testament area the Archaeological discoveries are fewer because the span of time covered is much less than that covered by the Old Testament."*[17]

An important term to keep in mind regarding archaeology is "Tell.' A 'tell' is the mound from continued building on a site of what is a no longer inhabited city. Such sites either have had some excavation or are a prospect for future excavation.

It used to be assumed that the authors of the New Testament were very mistaken or had merely made up much of the supposed history and other data they were presenting. However, archaeology has confirmed many hundreds of New Testament details and provided the basis for confidence in the accuracy of these writings.

As stated previously, archaeology cannot prove the New Testament documents to be the Word of God, but provides reasons for confidence that the writings were made in the first century and are reliable regarding the history, geography, peoples, and cultures of which it speaks. That provides a foundation for further consideration as to its origin or source.

You might wonder how the non-biblical manuscripts of the Dead Sea Scrolls could be valuable as to the New Testament. Some of those manuscripts verify the various Jewish sects and groups mentioned in the New Testament. Some of them inform us of messianic concepts of the time and give some parallels to doctrines and practices of prophecy used in the New Testament.[18]

One example of the benefit of archaeology is that most of the ancient cities mentioned by Luke in the book of Acts have been identified. Previously most of those cities were unknown outside of the Bible. Because of that, the critics had denied the existence of many of those cities. *"In all Luke names 32 countries, 54 cities, and nine Islands without error!*"[19]

A few skeptics claimed that Nazareth did not exist in Jesus' day because there are no known writings mentioning the village prior to the Gospels. However, Nazareth has been proven by archaeology to have been in existence during that time through discovery of structures and materials there dated to the first century.[20] The village population was approximately 400 people in the first century, so it should be no surprise that no prior historical references to it existed. [21]

Thomas Paine, in his book, The Age of Reason mentions that pagan mythology taught that many of their extraordinary men were reputed to be sons of a god. He also referred to the belief that those gods were said to have had sexual relations with human women.[22] From these examples, Paine then declared that the birth of Jesus as the Son of God was just a revised version of the pagan myth.

There are, however, significant differences between those stories. Each of the pagan stories involved sexual relations between the god and human. None of the other assumed births was declared to be of a virgin. Neither had any one of those other births been prophesied 500 years in advance.

Skeptics have many criticisms of the birth narratives of Jesus, especially stemming from the supernatural elements in the accounts. However, we have a valuable historical test available which most skeptics ignore or minimize. That test is based upon the fact that we have two independent birth accounts for Jesus. *"The vast majority of scholars, both conservative and liberal, believe that these writers were not familiar with each other's work. So, we can test the historical accuracy of Matthew by comparing it with Luke, and vice versa."* [23]

David van Biema wrote the cover story for the December 2004 issue of Time Magazine on the birth of Jesus. He stated *"And despite agreeing on the big ideas, Matthew and Luke diverge in conspicuous ways on the details."*[24] That is exactly what you would expect of two different authors writing independently regarding the same events!

Notice that they agree on the essentials and add complimentary and supplementary information in the details. Those details do not contradict each other but fill in further details regarding the events. In regard to these accounts, Roberts correctly states that, *"Different points and different perspectives do not constitute disagreement."* To repeat, none of the information in one account contradicts information in the other account.

Mark Roberts lists seventeen agreements in these two accounts of the information surrounding Jesus' birth from Matthew chapters 1-2 and Luke chapters 1-2:

1. His two human parents were Mary and Joseph. 2. Mary and Joseph were engaged, not yet married when Mary became pregnant. 3. Joseph was a descendant of king David of Israel. 4. Mary was still a virgin when she became pregnant. 5. The Holy Spirit was the source of Mary's conception. 6. News of Mary's pregnancy was unexpected and troublesome at first (to Mary in Luke and Joseph in Matthew). 7. Mary and Joseph remained a couple despite her premarital pregnancy. 8. An angel visited both parents to reveal the divine origin. 9. The angel gives the unborn baby the name Jesus. 10. Jesus is identified as the Savior by angels. 11. Jesus was born while Herod the Great was king of Judea. 12. Jesus was born in Bethlehem. 13 Jesus will be king of the Jews. 14. Jesus is the Messiah. 15. Jesus' birth was prophesied in Jewish Scriptures. 16. Unexpected visitors are summoned supernaturally to visit (Shepherds in Luke and Magi in Matthew). 17. Though born in Bethlehem, Jesus was raised in Nazareth.[25]

Roberts mentions that hyper-critical scholars might object that the early church made all this up. There is, however, no evidence to support such a contention. This is a case of the critics assuming and asserting what they prefer with no evidence to lend support to their contentions.

We are informed by Luke that Jesus' birth and life were begun during the rule of emperor Caesar Augustus who ruled Rome from 27 B.C. until 14 A.D. Matthew 2:1 informs us that Jesus was born during the rule of Herod the Great over Galilee and Judea. Inscriptions as well as the Jewish historian Josephus provide information on Herod. Herod received provisional rule over Galilee in 41 B.C., and later Judea and Samaria were added to his domain. He ruled these areas, first under Mark Antony and then Caesar Augustus until 4 B.C. when he died. Herod's existence and achievements are not challenged, neither is his reputation as ruthless, paranoid, and cunning.[26]

This verifies that Jesus was born by 4 B.C. or slightly before.[27] Josephus mentions that Herod died after a lunar eclipse and before the Jewish Passover that Spring. Most scholars accept the eclipse of 4 B.C. as the one to which Josephus referred. This further confirms that Jesus' birth was by 4 B.C.[28]

Excavations have revealed that Nazareth was a very small agricultural settlement in the first century. Caves for grain storage, cisterns as well as wine and olive presses date to Jesus' time. [29] It was at that time an insignificant village. Nazareth is located on a ridge, about 1200 feet above sea level in Galilee.[30] This location makes sense of the passage in Luke 5:28-29 which states the angry people of the synagogue led Jesus *"to the brow of the hill on which their city had been built, in order to throw Him down the cliff."*

It has been criticized that Rome was efficient and would not have required people to return to their birthplace in order to register for taxation because of the problems this would cause. However, a Roman census document records the testimony of a man stating that people mentioned earlier in the document have returned to his home for the census. This is regarding a census during the time of Emperor Claudius, approximately 48 A.D.[31] Other such census papyri are also known. Another example of requiring the return to one's family home is in regard to Egypt in 104 A.D.

"Gaius Vibius Maximus, Prefect pf Egypt: Seeing that the time has come for the house to house census, it is necessary to compel all those who for any cause whatsoever are residing out of their provinces to return to their own homes, that they may both carry out the regular order of the census and may also attend diligently to the cultivation of their allotments."[32]

Josephus refers to a census which would have occurred at 6 A.D. For this reason, it has been frequently declared that Luke 2:2 is mistaken in indicating that Quirinius was the governor of Syria at the time of Jesus birth (between 6-4 B.C.). The Greek word translated 'governor' is the same used in Luke 3:1 referring to Pontius Pilate but the two positions are not equivalent. The legate or governor was in charge of the entire province. Pilate was only over Judea (and Herod Antipas over Galilee). These were both part of the province of Syria. The word is not limited in meaning to governor. It can specify one who is ruling, governing, leading, or commanding.

Luke's account is stipulating that Quirinius was a ruler at Jesus birth in the Syrian Province of which Israel was a part. Quirinius had been in charge of Roman legions in Galatia, Cilicia and Syria and was probably the ranking military commander in Syria at the time of the census. Most likely, the legate at that time was Carius Sentius Saturninus. *"Roman records demonstrate that military officials oversaw and administered censuses, and Quirinius is even mentioned as a legate in the context of a census in Syria Province during the reign of Augustus.*"[33]

Quirinius held positions of high authority for Rome both military and civil. So, Luke is referring to the actual one in charge of the census in that province, who probably shared power with the provincial governor.

Additional discoveries have shown that a regular census was conducted in the Roman Empire every 14 years. Also, it is known from inscriptions and by Josephus that there were at least three and probably four people named Quirinius up through the second century A.D.[34]

The preaching and baptismal ministry of John the Baptist, as well as his influence on the common people is recorded by Josephus. In his book, <u>The Antiquities of the Jews</u>, Josephus also refers to John's arrest and execution by Herod.[35]

The location of Jesus birth as having been at Bethlehem has rarely been disputed. One exception was Joseph Smith who erroneously wrote in the book of Mormon about 1830 that Jesus was born in Jerusalem. Another example was a recent skeptic, who noted that Jesus' parents had been living in Nazareth prior to Jesus birth and that they returned there following their sojourn in Egypt. He asserted that Jesus was born in Nazareth which was why he was called Jesus of Nazareth.

This indicates that the skeptic denies the validity of the birth narratives, which tell where Jesus was born (Matthew & Luke). He also ignores or denies the references regarding the magi and Herod asking where the birth of Messiah was to occur and the answer from prophecy in Micah 5:2. The critic also ignores Herod's response of killing children in the area of Bethlehem out of paranoia and anger over the possibility of a rival. That critic displays the all-too-common practice of skeptics who often ignore much of the information we do have in order to assert their preferred opinions.

It is not likely that the tiny village of Bethlehem had an Inn during the first century. Though the word 'kataluma' can be translated inn, a different word, not used by Luke actually means inn. Luke uses 'kataluma' elsewhere to refer to an extra room in a house. The corrected reading of Luke 2:7 would be that there was 'no guest room available.' When Joseph and Mary arrived in Bethlehem, the extra room of

Joseph's family home was already occupied. With the influx of others back to their ancestral homes there was no other place for them.

They had to resort to a nearby cave in which Jesus was born. In first century, Israel, caves were often used for storage or to hold animals. Some argue that the cave was probably a lower level in a house where the animals were brought in at night. The manger (feeding trough) that the baby Jesus was placed into was built into the ground for the animals.[36]

Justin Martyr wrote in the second century A.D. that that when Joseph could not find lodging in the village of Bethlehem, he found a cave nearby and that while there Mary gave birth to the Christ.[37]

There were several facets to Roman opposition to the Christian faith. The most well-known is the frequent recurrence of persecution. However, there were also written attacks and opposition as well as attempts to obscure and destroy sites that were considered important and sacred to the followers of Jesus. *"Emperor Hadrian (reigned AD 117-138) even attempted to erase, defile, and syncretize the memory of the birth of Jesus by constructing a shrine to the god Adonis over the cave."*[38]

Emperor Hadrian sought to paganize everyplace thought to have been of early Christian significance. Where the cross was thought to have stood, he placed a marble statue of Venus, and a statue of Jupiter at the place thought to have memorialized the burial and resurrection.[39]

Hadrian's hostility may have actually resulted in preserving the site of the possible birth. Emperor Constantine had the Church of the Nativity erected over the site (completed in 339 A.D.). Skeptics have claimed the site to have originally been a cult site for Adonis taken over by Christians. However, it seems well attested that Jesus' birth was asserted to be there first and Hadrian slightly later having the shrine built there as part of his program to obscure the historical memory of Jesus and destroy Christianity.

Hadrian even went to the extreme of have a temple to Jupiter built on Mount Gerizim. That temple appears on Roman coins Under the remains of that temple for Jupiter are ruins of a building which was from about the 4th century B.C. These ruins may be that of the Samaritan temple. [40]

Celsus, a pagan Roman philosopher wrote against Christianity in the second century. In his <u>The True Word</u> he acknowledged Jesus' birth in a village of Judea, mentioned Mary and the story of Jesus' virgin birth. Celsus claimed that Jesus invented the virgin birth story because his mother had been convicted of adultery and that his actual father was a Roman soldier named Pantera.[41]

The Jerusalem Talmud repeats this story about 200 A.D. This explanation has sometimes been repeated by liberal theologians but has very little credibility because the only mentions of it are from enemies of Jesus. However, Celsus thus revealed that the belief in the virgin birth was known in Rome during the second century outside of Christian circles. It is significant that neither Jewish nor Roman sources dispute the birth of Jesus in a small Judean village.

There is no known confirmation of Joseph, Mary and Jesus escaping to Egypt. However, Egypt was easily accessible and there was a large Jewish population in Alexandria. It is possible the family may have had relatives there. Egypt was also free from any political connections with Herod, who did have connections in Syria and other nearby areas. So, it would have made sense to go to Egypt to escape Herod.

Critical scholars assert that Herod's slaughter of the children in the area of Bethlehem did not happen (Matt. 2:17-18). They assume it was propaganda against Herod and a falsified fulfillment of a prophecy by Jeremiah (31:5) or possibly a misunderstood interpretation of Herod's actual execution of his own sons. Such a slaughter, however, would have been consistent with Herod's character and there are early mentions or allusions to the slaughter.

A 1st-century Jewish apocryphal writing compares Herod to the pharaoh who had ordered the death of Hebrew male babies. This may be a reference to Herod's executing the children. Also, a 2nd-century apocryphal gospel does mention the executions by Herod.[42]

Matt. 2:20 mentions that *"those who sought the child's life are dead."* This implies more than just Herod was involved. The plural usage is best explained as referring also to Herod's son Antipater, who was also reputed to be cruel and likely involved in the murder of the young children in and around Bethlehem. Five days before his own death, Herod had murdered Antipater upon learning this son had rejoiced when he had thought his father to have died. Thus, both men probably involved in seeking to kill Jesus were dead.[43]

Though Jesus and Joseph are frequently called carpenters, the word 'tekton' can mean any type of craftsman. They were most likely to be primarily involved in stone masonry because of the shortage of wood and plentiful stones in the region.

Mark 5:35 uses the phrase 'ruler of the synagogue.' The phrase also occurs in the book of Acts. This has been proven to be a correct title. It was used commemorating the building of a first century synagogue in Jerusalem, as well as of later synagogue leaders at Chorazin and Caesarea Maritima. The synagogue ruler apparently oversaw the services, acted as a judge for the local community and as a patron of the synagogue. [44]

That Pilate was the ruler of Judea at the time of Jesus is verified by an inscription commissioned by Pilate on a limestone block at the theatre of the Roman capital city of Caesarea. This stone had been reused in the construction of the theatre. This was the first archaeological evidence of Pilate. [45]The inscription in Latin reads "Pontius Pilate, Prefect of Judea" and mentions dedication to Tiberius Caesar.

This verifies he was prefect of Judea prior to 41 A.D. The title was changed to Procurator after direct rule by Rome was reinstituted. According to Josephus Pilate ruled from 26 A.D. to 36 A.D. Pilate was also mentioned by the ancient historians Josephus, Philo, and Tacitus.

A ring with the Greek form of Pilate's name was excavated at the palace fortress of the Herodium near Bethlehem in a layer of first century artifacts and coins. Pilate's name Pilato is backwards on the ring as would be used to stamp documents.[46]

Evidence of the first century Temple of Herod where Jesus and the apostles taught and the early Christians worshipped is difficult to come by because of Muslim building on the site. However, a limestone slab was discovered by the French archaeologist Charles Clermont-Ganneau in 1871. The inscription is the same as that described by Josephus in the late first century. It reads *"No foreigner is to enter within the railing and enclosure around the temple. And whoever is* caught will be responsible to himself for his subsequent death."[47]

Herod the Great expanded the area of the temple complex significantly. Sections of the outer courts became used for the sale of animals for the sacrifices and changing money into the proper kind and denomination for the temple tax. According to the Mishnah, these financial transactions were made at extortionist prices.[48] Huge profits were made especially during the feast of Passover.

This indicates that Jesus cleansing of the temple was certainly warranted and necessary. There were apparently two occasions of Jesus driving out the sellers and money changers. One was at about the beginning of His ministry around 28 A.D. (John 2:13-17) and the other following the triumphal entry in 33 A.D. (Matt. 21:12-13; Mark 11:15-18; Luke 19:45-46).

A fragmentary second warning inscription was found outside the Old City of Jerusalem in 1935. These warnings explain the Jews hostility and intentions to kill Paul when they mistakenly assumed he had brought Trophimus the Ephesian into the Temple (Acts 21:28-29).[49]

Archaeologist Benjamin Mazar discovered a 3-foot-long stone in the midst of the rubble that must have been thrown down from the Temple Courts during the 70 A.D. destruction of the temple by the Romans. The incomplete reading states "To the place of trumpeting" which referred to the place where the priests would have blown the trumpets at the Temple to announce the beginning and ending of the Sabbath. Josephus described that location.[50] The stone weighs about eight tons. There is a niche in the stone where the priest would stand to blow the trumpet.[51]

This is significant as another verification that the Jewish temple had existed on that site in the first century. This was many centuries before the Muslim Mosque was built over the site of the destroyed temple.

Luke lists those who were rulers in nearby areas on behalf of Rome during the fifteenth year of Tiberius Caesar. This was when John the Baptist began his ministry (Luke 3:1). John is mentioned by the 1st century historian Josephus.[52] Pilate is listed as governor of Judea, and Herod [Antipas] as tetrarch of Galilee. Lysanias, said to be tetrarch of Abilene, is the most disputed of those listed. However, he is mentioned in both archaeological and ancient historical accounts. Josephus mentions him in connection with his domain in Abila.

Also, two 1st century inscriptions document this Lysanius as tetrarch during the time of Tiberius and Pilate. One inscription reads, *"Lysanius the tetrarch established this street and other things."* [53] The second inscription is a dedication of a temple "... *for the salvation of the Lord's Imperial and their whole household, by Nymphaeus a freedman of Lysanius the tetrarch."* [54] The confusion has been caused because of an earlier Lysanius who was executed by Mark Antony. The earlier Lysanius may have been the grandfather of this tetrarch.

Luke lists Philip as the brother of Herod [Antipas]. There are no known texts or inscriptions where Philip the tetrarch used the name of Herod. For that reason, it has been claimed by some scholars that Philip was not part of the Herodian dynasty. [55] Coins issued by him include his name and title as tetrarch. He is known to be a Herod because the domains of Herod the great were distributed to his three surviving sons, Herod Antipas, Archelaus and Philip.

Archelaus is only mentioned once in the entire New Testament (Matt. 2:22-23). When Joseph found that Archelaus had replaced Herod in ruling Judea he was afraid to settle there and returned to Nazareth instead. That makes sense as Archelaus developed a reputation as a violent and tyrannical ruler. Josephus recounted Archelaus' rule over Judea. Accusations by the Jews and Samaritans jointly, succeeded in his removal and banishment after ruling for nine years. [56]

Annas is documented as having been high priest from approximately 6-15 A.D. He was the father-in-law of the high priest Caiaphas (18-36 A.D.). Due to the lifetime appointment of high priests in the Mosaic law Annas was still considered a high priest among the Jews and held considerable influence (Num. 35:25-28; Luke 3:2; John 18:13, 24). This was despite Annas having been deposed by a previous Roman prefect, Valarius Gratus. [57] So it makes sense that Jesus was taken to Annas first after his arrest.

Caiaphas played a major role in having Jesus sentenced to death by Pilate. Ancient records and the Caiaphas family tomb, including inscribed ossuaries has been found proving he was quite prominent in the first century.[58] That ossuary of Caiaphas was the first evidence regarding Caiaphas outside of the New Testament.[59]

John mentions a healing by Jesus to have taken place at the pool of Bethesda (John 5:2). John mentions the strange situation of the pool having five porticoes. Porticoes were like covered porches on different sides of the pool. This pool was rediscovered near the end of the 19th century by archaeological excavation. The unusual feature of a fifth portico resulted from the pool being extended in one direction essentially creating twin pools with a fifth portico forming a division between the upper and lower pools.[60] So John was accurate.

It has been suggested that the 'troubling of the water' at the pool of Bethesda (Jn. 5:7) may have been caused by some feature of the connecting channels of water for the two pools or even "the existence of an intermittent spring like the Gihon spring." [61]

The memory of the healing at the pool of Bethesda had obviously persisted. As a part of the 2nd century emperor Hadrian's efforts to defile or remove evidence of Jesus, he had a shrine to Asclepius, the Greek god of healing built at the southside of the pools. The association with Asclepius was confirmed by the discovery of an exquisite Roman period vase decorated with snakes near the pools. Asclepius was associated with snakes by his snake entwined staff and rituals.[62]

In Mark 16:3-4 Women on the way to the tomb of Jesus to anoint his body question among themselves, "Who will roll away the stone for us from the entrance to the tomb?" They arrive to find it has already been rolled away. These statements suggest a stone of the correct size and shape that would be rounded so as to cause a tight seal of the tomb's entrance that would be rolled into place. There have been a number of tombs found in Judea from the Roman era that were closed by the means of a 'cartwheel' stone that had to be rolled into place.[63]

Ancient writings and excavated artwork have depicted 1st century Galilean boats. However, in January of 1986 a boat was discovered between the harbors of two coastal towns from the first century. The water level of the Sea of Galilee had substantially declined from a drought revealing this boat encased in mud. The measurements of the boat were about 26.5 feet in length, 7.5 feet in width and the height was preserved up to 4.5 feet. [64]

Pottery found in the boat, analysis of the nails used in construction and radiocarbon tests have concluded the boat was in use between the years of approximately 50 B.C. and 50 A.D. The boat gave evidence of many repairs over long use. Josephus had recorded that these boats were capable of carrying 15 people or more. So, this type of boat would have been easily capable of holding Jesus and the twelve.

On the northwestern shore of the Sea of Galilee lies Capernaum. Luke 4:31-38, Mark 1:21 and John 6:59 each mention the synagogue at Capernaum where Jesus taught. Ruins of a black basalt synagogue that dates to the first century has been found beneath a fourth and fifth century synagogue there. The walls are somewhat out of line with the synagogue above it proving it was not merely the foundation for the later synagogue. This is almost certainly the synagogue in which Jesus preached.[65]

Coins and pottery prior to the first century A.D. found under the structure help to date the ruins to the first century. The thickness of the walls ensure that it was not a private home, and as mentioned it was obviously not the foundation for the more recent structure.[66] A first century home has also been found in Capernaum. There is speculation that it might be the home of the apostle Peter, but there does not seem to be any way to actually prove this.[67]

Capernaum was in the same area as Magdala and near Tabgha. Josephus mentions it and its location.[68] Located on several major roads as well as at the Sea of Galilee made it an important commercial center for fishing, agriculture, and trade. Excavations have shown it to be primarily a fishing village as the Gospels portray. The existence of tax collectors and Roman customs house also gave evidence of Capernaum's importance. (Matt. 17:24; Mark 2:2-14).[69]

The city of Capernaum was a significant center of Jesus' Galilean ministry. Capernaum was located by Sea of Galilee in the region of Zebulun and Naphtali according to Matt. 4:13. Zebulun was immediately west of the Sea of Galilee according to Josh 19. In the 1st century Josephus had an accident near the mouth of the Jordon. He was taken to the nearby village which was certainly Capernaum, according to references Josephus made in his <u>Life</u>. The ancient remains of Capernaum are now known as Tell Hum.[70]

Jesus gave the sermon on the mount, at a location near Capernaum according to Matthew 5. However, a similar discourse reported in Luke is said to be on a level place after descending a mountain (Luke 6:17-49). Critics assume this to be an error or contradiction. There are at least two possible resolutions. The mountain could mean the mountainous area rather than on a particular mountain. It is also likely that these are two separate occasions. The content varies and the Luke version is much shorter than that of Matthew which suggests this may be a repetition of a previous sermon.

Magdala is mentioned only once in the Gospels (Matt. 15:39). It is assumed from her name, that Mary Magdalene was from this town. Magdala was south of Capernaum at the sea of Galilee and north of Tiberias. It was a center of fishing as evidenced by a structure with various tanks for a variety of kinds of fish and a site for tying up fishing boats. There was also the nearby discovery of a first century fishing boat mentioned elsewhere in this publication. [71]

Magdala was destroyed between 66-70 A.D. during the first Judean revolt against Rome. Death and slavery resulted for thousands of the inhabitants and the town never completely recovered.[72] A well preserved first century synagogue has been discovered near the main entrance to the city.[73]

The city of Tiberias is also only mentioned once in the Gospels (Jn. 6:23), though the ruler of Galilee who resided there (Herod Antipas) is mentioned numerous times. Antipas began construction of his new capital about 18 A.D. and named it in honor of Tiberias, the current emperor. It was populated with soldiers, wealthy - who were friendly to Rome - and poor from outside the area. The population was likely about 40,000.

Herod Antipas is known for the arrest and execution of John the Baptist (Matt. 14:6-11). Josephus refers to Herod Anitipas and to that event.[74] This Herod was referred to by Jesus as a ceremoniously unclean animal, a fox (Luke 13:31-33). A few rare coins from his era also mention Herod Antipas as "Herod the Tetrarch."[75]

For a few years around 30 A.D., Agrippa I was apparently appointed market overseer of Tiberias. This is confirmed by

Josephus and a weight inscribed with such information found there. The city sided with Rome during the first Judean revolt and was spared. [76]

Stone vessels were commonly used for ritual purposes in Judea and Galilee. According to the Law of Moses stone did not become ritually unclean as did other pottery. John 2:6 mentions six large stone jars for ritual cleansing. These vessels were of various quality and size which was why John states the six water pots varied in content. Usually, they were from approximately 26 to 32 inches in height with a diameter of 16 to 20 inches. John says they were from 2-3 *metretas* which would amount to around 9 gallons.[77]

Jesus told the crowd and his disciples to obey the teachers of the law and the Pharisees because they sit in Moses seat (Matt. 23:2). This was a reference to their religious authority. The seat of Moses was an actual stone bench or chair in the synagogue, reserved for distinguished leaders or the synagogue ruler. One of these seats was found in the ruins of Chorazin.[78]

The animosity between the Jews and Samaritans we find in the Gospels was of long standing. Following the conquest of Israel in 722 B.C. Assyria moved Assyrians and others into the territory of Israel. Babylon repeated that system when they conquered Judea. Intermarriage of these people with the remnant of Jews left in the land gradually developed a distinct people group who became known as Samaritans. The Samaritans combined worship of Yahweh with their prior religions.

When the Jews were allowed to return to Israel following the decree of Cyrus, they refused to allow the Samaritans to participate in rebuilding the temple at Jerusalem. This resulted in animosity and competition between the two groups. *"Conflicts between the people of Judea and the people of Samaria been going on for hundreds of years, and this continued into the 1st century AD."*[79]

Samaria was in between Galilee and Judea. When Galileans came to Jerusalem for the festivals and other religious ceremonies, Josephus said they normally traveled through Samaria which was the most direct route. That route only took three days.[80]

The Samaritans built their own temple on Mount Gerizim and established their own priesthood. [81] They made slight modifications to the Torah designating that, that location was the holy mountain and their temple was the true one. This was the basis for the encounter between Jesus and the Samaritan woman at Jacob's well. She stated that "Our fathers worshipped on this mountain." (John 4:7-9, 20-21). [82] John mentions the town called Sychar near Jacob's well where Jesus and his disciples encountered a Samaritan woman and then the entire town. Sychar existed near the ruins of Shechem during Roman times. Materials from the first century have been recovered there. [83]

In John 9, Jesus applied a mud poultice to the eyes of a man born blind and sends him to the pool of Siloam to wash. As a result, the man is healed receiving sight. The location of that pool was unknown in modern times until rediscovered in 2004. Repairing a drainage system resulted in discovering two ancient stairs which then led to excavation and the pool's discovery about 20 steps below the current street level. [84] The pool is located at the end of Hezekiah's tunnel. [85]

A recent criticism I read was that if Jesus was really God, 'Why did God call him, His Son?' The confusion is as a result of not recognizing that the Bible teaches that Jesus was God and equal with God the Father from all eternity (Isaiah 9:6; John 1:1-3; Romans 1:3-4; Colossians 1:15-17; 1Timothy 2:5-6; Hebrews 1:1-3). But then one person of the Triune God, the Logos, took on a human existence (the incarnation) as Jesus the Messiah in addition to being God. So then, in his humanity, he became also the Son of God through His supernatural birth.

Caesarea Philippi was about 25 miles north of the Sea of Galilee. It was built by Phillip the tetrarch and first named after Caesar Augustus and the god Pan. (Caesarea Paneas). Later Phillip altered the second part of the name after himself (Caesarea Phillipi). [86] It was in an area deeply steeped in pagan worship. Multiple deities were worshipped there in the first century including Pan, Caesar Augustus, and Jupiter Olybraeus.

A large cave in the midst of the rock cliff consists of a deep cavern filled with water from a spring that also feeds the Jordon River. *"The massive cave that descended deep into the earth was even regarded by many pagans as a gateway to*

Hades and because of this, associations with the underworld were strong at the sanctuary."[87]

When Jesus and his disciples were at Caesarea Philippi, Jesus made this famous declaration in response to Peter's confession, "*And I also say to you that you are Peter, and upon this rock I will build my church; and the gates of Hades shall not overpower it." (Matt. 16:18).* This statement regarding the 'gates of hades' is so much more striking when we recognize the geographical context in which it was spoken! Later the name of the town gradually became called Panaes after the god Pan. In the fifth century the pagan sites there were abandoned because the government and people became so involved in Christianity.[88]

When the Pharisees and Sadducees plotted to kill Jesus, He avoided public appearances and stayed at the town of Ephraim near the wilderness (Jn. 11:47-54). The location is not definitely known. But it was mentioned in 1 Maccabees 11:27-34 (cf. 5:46); 2 Maccabees 12:27, and by Josephus, Wars 4:9.551.[89]

The miracles reported of Jesus in the New Testament are a major point of contention and contradiction in the mind of skeptics. It is significant that the enemies of Jesus in the first century never deny that a miracle was accomplished by Him. Instead, they fault Him for doing miracles on the Sabbath or attribute the miracle to the power of the devil. The early Roman opponent of Christianity, Celsus, acknowledged that Jesus did miraculous deeds but attributed them to Jesus having learned Egyptian magic.[90]

The Jewish Mishna compiled about 200 A.D. contains information from much earlier times. "*One passage in particular mentions how Jesus allegedly practiced sorcery or magic and led Israel astray, which is an obvious reference to the miraculous, supernatural works Jesus performed.*"[91] This is unintentional testimony by Jesus enemies that the miracles attributed to Jesus were not later additions to the text but were actually observed at the time!

The city of Jericho was destroyed at the beginning of the invasion of Canaan under Joshua (c. 1400). A newer city named Jericho had been built about a mile south of the destroyed city. Jericho is mentioned six times in the Gospels. Archaeological remains testify to this more recent city, and its existence in the first century is confirmed by the writings of 1 Maccabees 9:50,16:11-17; Geography by Strabo and Josephus' Antiquities. [92]

There is an alleged contradiction between Matt. 20, Mark 10 and the account in Luke 18:35-43 relating the healing of the blind man or men. The first two accounts say the event happened as Jesus was leaving Jericho while Luke says it was while approaching Jericho.

One possible solution is that Luke is saying it is the blind approaching Jericho but stopped to rest and beg (the Greek does not say Jesus but only "he"). Another possibility is that the verb translated 'was approaching' (in Luke) is often translated "being close" or "near" which may have been the correct translation here. That would apply for though Jesus was leaving Jericho he was still near the city.[93]

The small village of Bethphage was the source of the donkey Jesus rode into Jerusalem on his final return there. The exact location is not certain but it is between Bethany and Jerusalem, very close to Jerusalem. The village is mentioned numerous times in the Talmud. [94] This confirms another geographical detail in Jesus' life. Bethany was better known so the addition of it in Mark 11:1 and Luke 19:29 is likely made to aid in locating Bethphage.[95]

In John 10:11, 14 Jesus used the metaphors of a shepherd and sheep. He claimed to be the good shepherd of the sheep who were representing those who recognized and believed in Him. An interesting Christian sculpture from Egypt portrays Jesus as a shepherd carrying a lamb with two other lambs looking up to him. It is dated as 3rd century A.D.

Bethany was the location of the raising of Lazarus (John 11), and where Jesus was six days before the Passover (Jn. 12:1) Jesus taught in the temple and then returned to Bethany at night from Jerusalem prior to the final Passover and his arrest (Matt. 21:17-18, Mark 11:11-12). It was a little less than two miles from Jerusalem and has been proven to have been inhabited until about 100 A.D.[96]

The religion of Judaism was unique among all the religions of the peoples Rome conquered. The Jews refused the erection of pagan images and refused to worship Caesar. When taxes were increased and the assignment of the high priest was assumed by the Roman procurators the Jewish resentment toward Rome boiled over. A few rulers such as

Emperor Caligula and Pilate seemed to take pleasure in inciting the Jews.

When a large amount of silver was confiscated from the temple by the procurator Florus in 66 A.D., there was a riot in which the Roman garrison in Jerusalem was massacred. Troops were sent from Syria which were also defeated. Rome responded by sending three legions totaling 60,000 troops. Prior to the siege of Jerusalem an estimated 100,000 Jews were killed or enslaved as the legions advanced. [97]

When the legions broke through the Jerusalem walls in 70 A.D. they tore down, destroyed, and burned everything within their reach. The huge stones Herod had used to build the temple walls destroyed the street below as they were pushed off the temple mount.

A carved milestone was found near the temple area which mentions the emperor Vespasian and his son Titus, commander of the Roman army that suppressed this revolt. Rome was especially proud of their success at defeating this uprising and publicized their victory with coins, statues, and other monuments as well as written propaganda. A new tax was also imposed upon Judea.[98]

Critics declare that Jesus' words, "*not one stone here will be left upon another*' (Matt. 24:2) was not fulfilled because there are visible remains of some structures. However, the criticism is based upon a flawed interpretation. Jesus' words were in regard to the temple court buildings which the disciples had pointed out. It did not include the surrounding walls nor foundation stones. Part of the western wall and southern court were not even completed until 65 A.D.[99]

Skeptics allege a contradiction between Matthew's account, which mentions bringing the donkey and its colt, while the other three gospels only mention the colt which Jesus rode upon (Matt. 21:5-7; Mark 11:7; Luke 19:35; John 12:14-15). The resolution is that the other gospel writers focus only upon the colt since Jesus only rode the colt and that was the fulfillment of prophecy (Zech. 9:9).[100]

"*Jesus began the triumphal entry outside the boundaries of Jerusalem in Bethphage on the Mount of Olives, rode on a donkey like the kings of ancient Israel, descended down the road into the Kidron Valley, entered the city through the Susa Gate, then went to the temple where he cleansed it of* merchants and moneychangers. The similarities to the Roman Imperial triumph and the ancient Israelite kingship procession would have been obvious to the informed observer." [101] In this one procession Jesus carried out traditions associated with both ancient kings, conquering victors as well as the divine.[102]

The Susa Gate, in earlier times called the Eastern Gate, was in the first century the only gate on the eastern side of the Jerusalem temple complex. This was the gate of access from the Mount of Olives. Ezekiel 44:1-3 stated that God would enter the temple through the Eastern Gate. Geography, as well as prophecy indicate this to be Jesus' entry point to the temple and city. During the Byzantine Christian era the Eastern Gate began to be called the Golden Gate.[103]

East of Jerusalem across the Kidron Valley on the lower northwestern slope of the Mount of Olives is the Garden of Gethsemane. There are still many ancient olive trees in the vicinity though none are more than 1000 years old. All the original trees from Jesus' time were cut down by Roman general Titus for use in the Roman siege of Jerusalem in 70 A.D.[104] Descriptions in the Gospels, early Christian writings and a Byzantine Church constructed there have enabled us to identify the location of Gethsemane almost 2000 years later.[105]

Mark seems to disagree with the other Gospel accounts of Peter's denial of Jesus. Matthew records Jesus stating, *"Truly I say to you that this very night, before a cock crows, you shall deny me three times."* (Matt. 26:34). The fulfillment of Jesus words is recorded following Peter's third denial: *"And immediately a cock crowed. And Peter remembered the word which Jesus had said, Before a cock rows, you will deny me three times."* (24:74-75).

Mark, however reads, *"And Jesus said to him, Truly I say to you, that you yourself this very night, before a cock crows twice, shall three times deny me."* (Mark 14:30). The fulfillment is stated, *"And immediately a cock crowed a second time, and Peter remembered how Jesus had made the remark to him, 'Before a cock crows twice, you will deny me three times."* (14:72). Luke and John agree with Matthew which makes Mark's account seem like a contradiction. However, it is not the problem it may seem.

There are two possible resolutions, The first is that Mark is merely giving more details than the other accounts. This would be natural as Mark is writing under the influence and from the perspective of Peter. As a major character in the event, it would not be unusual for Peter to add more detail.[106] Another and related resolution is that Jesus made both statements. It may be that as Peter continued to insist that he would not deny Jesus, Jesus repeated the alternate statement. There is no genuine problem.[107]

The night of Jesus' arrest in the Garden of Gethsemane Luke 22:44 mentions that Jesus' anxiety was so great that his sweat became 'like drops of blood.' Though very rare, this condition, known as hematidrosis can occur from extreme stress. It was mentioned by Aristotle, and a few others in ancient times. That none of the other Gospels mention this detail during Jesus' anguish is readily explained by the fact that Luke was a medical doctor.[108]

According to John 18:12-24 Jesus was apparently taken to the home of Annas then to that of Caiaphas. The home of the high priest appears to have been a central location for the religious leadership in addition to the Sanhedrin meeting place at the temple complex.[109]

Judas, in remorse, returned the thirty pieces of silver which he had obtained for betraying Jesus. The chief priests stated the money could not be deposited in the temple treasury because it was blood money. They purchased the Potter's Field as a burial place for strangers (Matt. 27:6-8). Excavations show that it did indeed become a burial place for foreigners during about the mid-1st century. That the field was not used for burial until about the middle of the first century is confirmed by radiocarbon tests.[110]

Mark 15:16 and Matthew 27:27 mentions Jesus being taken into the Praetorium, the Roman Palace in Jerusalem. John 19:13 mentions that Pilate sat at the judgment seat, or gabbatha, and wrote the sentence for Jesus' crucifixion. Gabbatha means height, raised place or ridge. This raised platform and part of the 1st century courtyard of the Praetorium has been excavated.[111]

Though the Sanhedrin was determined that Jesus be executed, they had lost the power to carry out capital punishment in 6 A.D. when Rome took over direct control of Judea. The only exception was if a foreigner violated the prohibition against going into the temple. Otherwise, the Jewish council had to obtain the decision of the Roman prefect, (Pilate in this case) for the death penalty to be legally carried out.[112]

Pilate seems uncharacteristically weak before the demands of the Sanhedrin during his trial of Jesus. His reputation was of being ruthless and domineering. Why was he different this time? Pilate was attempting to avoid angering the Jewish religious leaders, because it would endanger his position and status with Emperor Tiberias. He was in a precarious position because Tiberias had recently arrested the powerful commander of his Praetorian guard, Lucius Sejanus for treason and executed many of the commander's associates. It is thought that Pilate had actually been appointed by Sejanus at his peak of power rather than by Tiberias.[113]

Pilate had, had several serious conflicts with the Sanhedrin and the Jewish people previously. Also, Pilate had been chastised by Tiberias following one of those conflicts which had occurred after the fall of Sejanus.[114] The trial of Jesus was approximately 18 months after Sejanus' fall so Pilate needed to avoid any further negative attention from the emperor. Pilate even sent Jesus to Herod, hoping Herod would make the decision, and thus extricate him from the danger of his situation.

That sensitive situation is thought to be the basis of the fear aroused in Pilate when he sought to release Jesus and the Jews shouted, *"If you release this man, you are no friend of Caesar's; everyone who makes himself out to be a king opposes Caesar."* (John 19:12). Pilate quickly submitted to their will following that declaration.[115]

Celsus in The True Word recorded that Pilate suffered nothing for condemning to death a supposed god.[116] This would appear to be a reference to Pilot's action in having Jesus crucified. Pilate was not held accountable by any human authority for that miscarriage of justice.

As mentioned previously, outside the Bible, there are about half a dozen various non-Christian writings referring to Jesus in the late first and second centuries. These are given in Appendix A. In addition, there is an inscription on an ossuary only decades after Jesus' death and resurrection that may be a reference to Jesus. The ossuary is from 70 A.D. or before.

The inscription translated from Aramaic reads *"James, son of Joseph, brother of Jesus."*[117]

Though all three of the names were very common in first century Israel, *"there is no other known James, son of Joseph, brother of Jesus."* [118] About 1,000 ossuaries are known from this period and approximately 25% have inscriptions. Of these, a brother is mentioned only one other time suggesting this "Jesus" was very significant.

This ossuary came from a tomb in Jerusalem, is carved from Jerusalem limestone and dates prior to the destruction of Jerusalem. This may be the burial box of James, Jesus' half-brother, and former leader of the Church, who was stoned to death in 62 A.D. by orders of the high priest Annas according to Josephus. [119] If so, it is the earliest artifact mentioning Jesus of Nazareth that is known.

Many ancient nations had used various forms of crucifixion for punishment prior to the Romans. Nations utilizing crucifixion earlier included the Assyrians, Carthaginians, Persians, and Greeks. It was, however, made into a science and powerful political weapon by Rome. *"The words cross and crucify are derived from the Latin crux, meaning cross, tree, or stake on which a person was impaled, hanged or executed, although the verb crucify was originally used to refer more generally to torture or execution."*[120]

The Greek equivalent word is stauros. These words did not specify a particular type of cross or stake. The Romans used crucifixion on a massive scale. *"The Romans typically used a vertical pole with a beam across the top (patibulum), appearing like a Latin T, or a vertical pole with an intersecting crossbeam, which according to early iconography associated with Christianity seems to have been the type used in the crucifixion of Jesus."*[121] Roman crucifixions were normally outside of a city or military camp along a major road so as to achieve maximum effect on the public.[122]

Following approval of the sentence of crucifixion, the convicted would be flogged with a flagellum or rods. There were other forms of torture which often severely weakened or even killed the condemned before they were nailed to the cross. [123] The crossbeam, weighing up to 100 pounds was required to be carried by the condemned, if they were able.

Those being crucified were either stripped naked or nearly so.[124]

The place of Jesus' execution is called Golgotha in Aramaic and means the place of a skull. There are related words in Hebrew meaning a wheel, round shape, and skull. Calvary is the equivalent word in Latin. In ancient writings this hill was not identified as resembling the face of a skull, but of the top of a skull. In addition, the four Gospels each refer to the hill with the Greek word Kranion referring to the cranium, the skull's upper rounded part.

The identification of a rocky escarpment as Golgotha, made in 1883 by Charles Gordon because of a semblance of a skull face is erroneous, despite an ancient tomb nearby. The site has acquired its present shape from severe erosion as a result of modern quarrying. [125] Additionally, there is no evidence of a garden having been nearby. The traditional site (from at least the 4th century) of Jesus' execution is covered by the Church of the Holy Sepulchre. That site on a hill was outside the city walls of the first century, but near to a gate and road which was easily visible. The probable hill now is inside the city because of additional walls expanding with the growth of the city about 44 A.D. and a further extension in the 16th century.[126]

Some critics have contended that ropes were used to hold the victim's arms to the cross rather than nails as the bones in the hand would not bear the body's weight hanging on the cross. After the resurrection when Jesus said see my hands and my feet (Luke 24:39) he was definitely not referring to rope burns.[127]

The Jews considered the wrist as part of the hand and the bones in the wrist and legs can support the weight of the body. In fact, as mentioned below a crucified man from the Roman era has been found with a nail still lodged between the bones of one wrist and another man with the nail still in his heel bone. Thomas stated *"Unless I see the imprint of the nails in his hands and put my finger into the place of the nails … I will not believe."* (Jn. 20:25).

It is significant that the nails were not the cause of death by crucifixion. There were some different and inter-related causes, but the two most common causes were hypovolemic shock and asphyxia resulting from exhaustion.[128]

Another assumption of skeptics is that the description of the tomb of Jesus in the Gospels is wrong (Matt. 27:59-60; Mark 15:46). Amos Kloner, an Israeli archaeologist has examined more than 900 rock-cut tombs. Only four of these discovered tombs dating to the time of Jesus were closed by a rolling stone. These four had a slotted groove carved to one side of the tomb entrance. A heavy carved disk-shaped stone weighing several tons would be rolled into the slot after placing the body inside. Moving the stone would require several people.[129]

Such tombs were rare, only afforded by the wealthy or royalty. Joseph, as a member of the Sanhedrin was one of those people. Regarding Jesus' burial and the biblical text, *"The kind of tomb and sealing stone implied in the text fit the archaeological data described above."* This is seen as a fulfillment of Isaiah 53:9 *"He was assigned a grave with the wicked, and with the rich in his death."*[130]

An additional criticism is that since Joseph closed the tomb by himself, it must not have been a tomb of this type. However, though Joseph initiated obtaining the body, wrapping it in linen, and placing Jesus into the tomb, it does not mean he acted alone. He would have required assistance with each of these steps, so the criticism is invalid.

There are skeptical scholars who contend that Jesus body would have been dumped in a common grave with other executed criminals rather than receiving a traditional Jewish burial. They claim the report of his burial in the garden tomb to be mere fiction. However, Jesus was not a common criminal. He had loyal caring followers even after his conviction and crucifixion. Also, as a following paragraph indicates, some executed as criminals were still given typical Jewish burials.[131] This refutes the skeptics theory regarding Jesus' burial.

Graves of the wealthy like that in which Jesus was buried have been discovered in the area of Jerusalem.[132] The vast majority of graves from the Roman era in Judea were disturbed prior to opportunities for archaeological investigation. However, the skeletal remains of two crucified men from the Roman era in Judea confirm the use of nails.

One man, whose bones were found in an ossuary, still had the nail through the heal bone and his legs had been broken. The other man still had a nail lodged between the wrist bones of one hand.[133]The crucified could be given to relatives for burial or funeral rites once confirmed dead or could end up in a mass grave for criminals.[134] It is significant that these two crucified individuals were given a normal Jewish burial, so claims that Jesus would not have a had such a burial are refuted.

The so-called 'Nazareth Inscription' was acquired for a private collection in 1878. It was translated and published in 1930 after being obtained by the Paris National Library. The academic community was excited over this inscription. It was an edict of Caesar, probably Claudius (41-54 A.D.), apparently aimed at the Jewish community in Israel. The edict imposed the death penalty for anyone in Israel caught moving bodies from family tombs particularly from 'sepulcher-sealing tombs' which was the type Jesus was placed into. Attempts by critics to dismiss the connection of the inscription with Israel and Jesus lack credibility.[135]

This edict is extremely unusual in that it refers to the removal of the body. While grave robbing was a frequent occurrence in ancient times, the robbers were always after any valuables buried on or with the body. They were never interested in the body itself. This appears to be a case where Caesar heard of the claim of the resurrection and the Jewish leader's explanation that the disciples stole Jesus' body.

Some pseudepigraphal[136] and Gnostic books such as the Gospel of Mary and Gospel of Phillip constructed the idea that Jesus loved Mary Magdalene more than He did the apostles. More recently some skeptics have surmised that Jesus and Mary were married and had children. Then during construction at the Talpiot section of Jerusalem in 1980 ten ossuaries (limestone bone boxes) were discovered dating between approximately 1st century B.C. and the end of the 1st century A.D.

Little interest resulted from the discovery until a documentary was made attempting to prove the tomb was of Jesus of Nazareth and his family. Despite *"Supposedly indicated by ossuary inscriptions, geology and DNA, this hypothesis fails when scrutinized."*[137]

As archaeologist Titus Kennedy remarks, *"However, nearly all scholars have disagreed with this hypothesis, regardless of their worldview, because those conclusions stretch and even conflict with the data."* [138] One issue is that though the name Jesus was very common, it does not occur in these ossuaries, and the names which do appear, Mary, Martha, Joseph, Judas, and Matthew were also extremely common in 1st century Israel.[139]

Additional arguments against the film's assumptions were that the unknown son of Joseph did not share DNA with the Marianne or other possible mother in the ossuary and there were no ancient Christian markings at the Talpiot tomb.[140]

The filmmakers later sought to link another ossuary that is inscribed *"James son of Joseph brother of Jesus"* with the Talpiot tomb to strengthen their claims. However, the James ossuary was purchased in the 1970's, years before the Talpiot tomb was uncovered and was from the Silwan area not Talpiot. Finally, it was never regarded that the James ossuary included or was that of Jesus.[141]

Added to the pretensions of having found the tomb of Jesus is a small fragment found in Egypt at the antiquities market. It was published and contains the words, *"Jesus said to them my wife..."* Initially this was accepted by some scholars as an authentic ancient text. More recently, a growing majority of scholars have agreed it was a forgery.

Two or more recent independent assessments have concluded the fragment appears to have copied and rearranged sentences and phrases from a modern translation of the Gnostic Gospel of Thomas and possibly other ancient Gnostic writings.[142] The ink and papyrus material are from the 7th or 8th century, if not fraudulently created using an ancient papyrus fragment and techniques to recreate ancient ink. Either way it is not of historical value or significance because of its Gnostic sources and late date.[143]

There has been extensive controversy as to the burial place of Jesus. The traditional site, is called "Gordon's tomb" because of the promotion of the site from 1883 by Charles Gordon. This location has the aesthetic appeal of being located in a beautiful garden but does not fit with the archaeological evidence.[144]

Finnegan gives details of Hadrian's effort in the second century to obscure the traditional burial site of Jesus. Hadrian buried the sepulcher and covered the entire area with a large amount of earth, covered that over with a stone pavement and the erected a shrine of Venus on top.[145] This may have actually preserved the knowledge of the correct site, contrary to Hadrian's intent.

"So it is evident that Hadrian carried out a systematic profanation of the shrines of the Jews and the Christians ... he must have selected the place of Calvary for such treatment on the basis of a traditional identification which long antedated his own time and thus reached back into the earliest periods of the Christian movement."[146]

Constantine built the Church of the Holy Sepulchre in Jerusalem at the probable site of Jesus' burial in the early 4th century. [147] *"Archaeological and early Christian literary evidence tend to further substantiate the Church of the Holy Sepulchre as standing at the burial site."*[148]

A visual distortion of the execution of Jesus was discovered at Palatine Hill, Rome in 1857. Jesus is portrayed as a donkey being executed on a cross. This bit of graffiti was carved into stone. The accompanying inscription has been translated as *"Alexamenos worships (his) God."* [149] Dated variously between 50 and 250 A.D., this graffiti presents one early pagan idea of Jesus. It does also unintentionally show that Jesus was worshipped as God by early Christians and is an early witness to the crucifixion of Jesus.

There were many spurious 'Gospels' written in the 2nd to 4th centuries. The so-called Gospel of Judas is one example of these writings with Gnostic and fictional characteristics. It begins with the statement: *"the secret account of the revelation that Jesus spoke in conversation with Judas Iscariot."* [150] This writing presents Judas as the greatest of Jesus disciples and the hero of the story rather than the villain (Matt. 26:14-16, 25).

Judas is said to have really understood Jesus' teachings, in contrast to the others. He is said to comprehend that Jesus came from *"the immortal realm of Barbelo."* Judas is further declared to have been privately tutored by Jesus and instructed that he would sacrifice Jesus thus becoming the hero. He alone is said to have understood the true gospel.[151]

This was written between 220-320 A.D. Rejection of the writing's authenticity is not only based upon being written too late and contradicting the much earlier eyewitness testimony. It also betrays its Gnostic origins by reference to the realm of Barbelo, (an assumed emanation from God) as well as claiming secret and private teaching of Judas by Jesus. The value of 'Judas' is that it and other Gnostic writings illustrate the kind of fictional and mythological writing of the early centuries of this era. Those writings contrast greatly with the straightforward character of the authentic Gospels.

There has been some controversy by skeptical authors and scholars over whether Jesus was married or not. This has been based upon certain Gnostic texts declaring that Jesus was married to Mary Magdalene. However, when Paul defended his right to have a wife (1Cor. 9:5), he mentioned that the other apostles had wives as did the brothers of the Lord and Cephas (Peter). Had Jesus been married, it would have clenched Paul's argument to have mentioned that example; so, no, Jesus was not married. [152]

History And Archaeological Evidence
Regarding The Book of Acts

In the past, skeptics, including liberal theologians, claimed that the book of Acts was a hopelessly unreliable and inauthentic writing of the mid-second century. However, the accuracy of Luke's statements has been repeatedly confirmed by archaeological discoveries, such as terms in the apostolic writings that appear in first century inscriptions, references to specific persons, and the identification and excavation of cities and provinces of the Roman world to which they make mention.[153]

William Ramsay had been convinced of the unreliability of the book of Acts by his professors. He began his work as an archaeologist with a profoundly anti-biblical perspective. However, once on the field and actually doing excavations, he was surprised to find his professors were sadly out of touch with reality.

Ramsay's research found that in case after case Luke was vindicated as accurate in his statements and descriptions. He found the archaeological evidence supported Luke rather than the skeptics. "*The more Ramsey encountered the Greco-Roman world (including archaeological descriptions of cities, customs, terms, and religious practices), the more he started using the New Testament as a guide he could rely on as he did his work.*"[154] He realized that Acts had to have been written in the mid-first century and was historically reliable. He also concluded that Luke should be considered a top-rate historian.[155]

The total transformation in Ramsey's perspective is expressed in the following statement: *"Our hypothesis is that Acts was written by a great historian, a writer who set himself to record the facts as they occurred, a strong partisan indeed, but raised above partiality by his perfect confidence that he had only to describe the facts as they occurred, in order to make the truth of Christianity and the honor of Paul apparent."*[156]

In Acts 4:33-39 Gamaliel a famous rabbi cautions the Sanhedrin as to their intention to kill the apostles. He reminds them of a previous movement led by Theudas, which following his death quickly dissipated. Josephus mentions Theudas having claimed to be a prophet and having gained a large following. Theudas was captured and beheaded and his movement fell apart as Luke mentions.[157]

Caesarea Maritima was the Roman capital of Palestine. This city lies on the Mediterranean coast halfway between modern Tel Aviv and Haifa. It was built by Herod the great from the ground up, taking ten or twelve years to complete. This new city was dedicated by Herod, at completion to Caesar.[158] Though not mentioned in the Gospels it was very important during the 1st century. It is mentioned frequently in the days of the early church, from Acts 8:40 on. Maritima was added to the name to distinguish it from the many other Roman cities named Caesarea.[159]

In his Natural History (vs. 14, 69) Pliny wrote a brief history of Caesarea calling it the "Tower of Strato". Josephus mentions it as the Roman headquarters calling it "Straton's Tower."[160] The city was given to Herod the Great by Caesar Augustus. Herod did extensive building there and named it Caesarea in honor of Augustus.[161]

Herod built an aqueduct about 13 miles long to supply water to his new city. Another of Herod's projects at Caesarea Maritima was the creation of an artificial harbor, probably the first in history.[162] He used an ancient technology, only recently rediscovered, of a special concrete that hardened underwater. Paul made use of this harbor on at least four occasions (9:30, 18:22, 21:8, 27:2).

Acts 11:20 mentions Jewish Christians fleeing persecution, going to Antioch in Syria. They began sharing the Gospel with Gentiles as well as Jews. This city of probably about three hundred thousand, had, according to Josephus, an unusually large Jewish population in the first century. These Jews had beautifully decorated synagogues and had attracted multitudes of Greeks to their monotheism.[163] That fits with the large numbers coming to Christ, the long ministry of Barnabas and Paul there and the establishing of Antioch as the home base for evangelism to the Gentiles.

Acts 11:28 mentions the prophet Agabus predicting a severe famine which is said in the verse to have happened during the reign of Emperor Claudius. A shortage of food in the empire during the reign of Claudius is mentioned by Suetonius, (Claudius, 18); Tacitus, (Annuals 12.43); Cassius Dio (History of Rome, 60.1); Josephus, (Antiquities 3.320-321, 20.2.5, 20.5.20). Papyri dated about 46 A.D, during Claudius' reign, indicate high grain prices and efforts to aid Jews with Egyptian grain during this famine by Queen Helena of Adiabene.[164]

Acts 12:19-23 Luke records the death of Herod Agrippa following his final speech in Caesarea Maritima. Josephus also refers to this event following Herod's speech giving more details including that stricken with violent abdominal pains, he died five days later.[165]

Barnabas and Saul took the first missionary journey at the behest of the Holy Spirit. Their first destination was the Island of Cyprus (Acts 13). At Paphos Barnabas and Saul met the proconsul Sergius Paulus and led him to faith. Paulus is thought to be mentioned as one of the authorities by the Roman historian, Pliny the Elder in Naturalis Historia.

There is also an inscription discovered at Soli near Paphos that mentions "the Proconsul Paulus" as well as other inscriptions suggesting he held other positions within the Roman Empire.[166] Some scholars distrusted Luke's accuracy in mentioning a proconsul in Cyprus, but the inscriptions have proven Luke to have been correct.[167]

A significant population of diaspora Jews resided in Phrygia in the 1st century.[168] After being driven out of Pisidian Antioch by antagonistic Jews, Paul and Barnabas went to Iconium (Acts 13:51). The presence of Jews in the Phrygian city of Iconium seems to be confirmed by inscriptions which would explain the presence of a synagogue (Acts 14:1). At the instigation of the Jews, they continued to be persecuted from city to city. That the persecution of Christians was common during the first two centuries in Phrygia is confirmed by ancient sources. [169]

Lystra is mentioned as one place Paul and Barnabas went after fleeing Iconium (Acts 14:6). Healing a man lame from birth, they were mistaken for Zeus and Hermes and a priest of Zeus sought to offer sacrifices to them, which they stopped (14:8-12). This event fits precisely with the religious culture of Lystra. Zeus was especially revered there and the oft regarded messenger of Zeus was also familiar to these people. Zeus had a local temple and the dedication of a statue of Hermes and of a sundial to Zeus has been found. Also found there is a stone alter dedicated to Zeus and Hermes as well as a portrayal of Hermes with the Eagle of Zeus.

The Roman author Ovid, familiar with this region wrote a story about 8 A.D. *"taking place in nearby Phrygia in which the gods Zeus and Hermes appeared in human form and went to 1,000 homes in the area seeking hospitality. However, only the elderly couple Philemon and Baucis were hospitable to the disguised gods and for this they were spared from the wrath of a flood that destroyed the valley and its people."*[170] It was approximately 40 years later when Paul's words led to the healing of the lame man as demonstration that he and Barnabas were sent by God that the people assumed this was Hermes and Zeus in person.

Paul and Barnabas were caught by surprise as the people communicated their misperception in the local Lycaonian language. Interpreters have questioned the reliability of this as to being an actual language. However, inscriptions throughout the region and a 6th-century encyclopedic book mention a Lycaonian language.[171]

In Philippi, Paul and Silas were beaten and imprisoned (Acts 16:16-24). A small stone building near the town forum is thought to have been that prison since at least the fifth century. McRay includes an excellent picture.[172]

In Caesarea Maritima two mosaics of Romans 13:3 have been found as part of the floor in a public building. *"If you would not fear the authorities, do that which is good."* These are as ancient as some of the oldest New Testament manuscripts and thus important for comparison.[173]

Acts 18:1-2 mention Paul meeting Aquila and Priscilla who had come from Italy because the Emperor Claudius had commanded the Jews to leave Rome. Roman historian Suetonius and others refer to this event which occurred in 49 A.D. [174] Suetonius wrote *"Since the Jews constantly made disturbances at the instigation of Chrestus, he [Emperor Claudius in AD 49] expelled them from Rome."* [175] While a few scholars prefer to assume this is a particular Jew agitating in Rome, most agree this to be a reference to Christ and to conflict between Christians and Jews. [176]

In Acts 18:4, though Luke mentions a synagogue in Corinth, the existence of one there during the first century has been debated. Internal evidence in the passage is the mention of Jewish associates of Paul's there and the statement regarding circumcision (7:18-19) which would not make sense unless there were Jews.

The Jewish philosopher Philo provides external evidence of a Jewish community in Corinth at that time. Also, in the first century, Josephus, the Jewish historian wrote that six thousand Jews had been moved to the area of Corinth by emperor Vespasian. They were among those captured during the Jewish rebellion and were sent as slave labor to construct a canal across the isthmus. [177]

Added to the written records is an inscription that, though damaged, appears to be from the doorway of a synagogue and an uppermost part of a column with Jewish symbols menorah, palm branches and a citron. [178] So although the synagogue of Corinth has not yet been found there is sufficient evidence to know that Luke is correct in stating Paul *"reasoned in the synagogue, trying to persuade Jews and Greeks."*

History and Archaeological Evidence
The Letters and Revelation

Paul's letter to the Romans concludes with several greetings from Paul's friends in Corinth. One of the greetings reads *"Erastus, the city treasurer greets you"* (16:23). Archaeologists at Corinth in 1929 discovered a middle of the first century inscription near the theater on a large paving stone that reads *"Erastus, in return for his aedileship laid [this pavement] at his own expense."* An elected official named an aedile was one who maintained public buildings, kept the streets repaired, managed local games etc.[179]

This is almost certainly the same Erastus for several reasons. First the name is uncommon and not found elsewhere in Corinth. Second, about 50 A.D. is while Paul was in Corinth and when this pavement was laid. Third, the specific word Paul used to designate Erastus as treasurer, is the word used of Erastus in the inscription as a Corinthian aedile.[180]

For one and a half years Paul had ministered in Corinth *"But when Gallio was proconsul of Achaia, the Jews made an united attack on Paul and brought him before the tribunal"* (18:12). This would have been in mid-51 A.D. The tribunal or speaker's platform where Paul was brought has been excavated.[181] A group of nine fragments discovered at Delphi, Greece is known as the Gallio Inscription and the Delphi inscription. Written by the Emperor Claudius, it is in regard to guarding the cult of Apollo at Delphi. It refers to *"Junius Gallio, my friend and proconsul of Achaia."*[182]

We know Gallio served as Proconsul from mid-51 to mid-52 A.D. This is not only confirmation of Luke's writing but helps pinpoint the timing of much of Paul's ministry.

Critics have condemned Paul for writing about slavery and never condemning it. They also criticize him for telling slaves to obey their masters (Eph. 6:5-8; Col. 3:22; 1Tim. 6:1; Titus 2:9). Paul did not condemn slavery because his commission was not to attempt to reform Roman society but to win people to faith in Christ. Condemning slavery would have just raised an additional obstacle against the gospel.

For an example of how that would have worked, compare the reactions today toward Christians fighting to eliminate abortion. Both issues are important but making them the focus is largely counterproductive and focusing on secondary issues. What Paul did instead was to establish principles that undermined slavery. And, everywhere that Christianity became a strong influence in those early centuries, slavery was abolished or withered away. The primary issue is coming to God with faith and repentance.

Excavations in the Judean desert near the Khirbet ed-Deir monastery, east of Hebron, discovered a fifth or sixth century mosaic of part of 1Cor. 15:52-53 on the resurrection of believers.[183]

In Acts 19:8 It is mentioned that Paul boldly spoke of Christ in the synagogue for three months. No first century synagogue has yet been found but evidence of a Jewish community there has been discovered. These include a funeral monument, pottery and glass with menorahs displayed on them. Another interesting fact is that there is a cave high above the city, in which there is a painting of Paul, the virgin Mary and a believer know as Thecla. This is the earliest known painting of the apostle Paul. [184]

Paul spoke daily at the hall of Tyrannus in Ephesus for two years according to Luke (Acts 19:9). So far, no such designated hall has been found, though an inscription mentioning an auditorium has been discovered. Also, several inscriptions containing the name Tyrannus have been discovered showing the name was well known in Ephesus and elsewhere, so there is no reason to not accept Luke's account.[185]

Ephesus was the capital and a commercial center of the province of Asia in modern western Turkey. It was also the location of many religious cults and superstition. It was a center for the worship of Artemis, and the practice of magic was a prominent feature of the area. This verifies the statements in Acts 19:18-19. [186] *"Many of those who had believed kept coming, confessing and disclosing their practices. And many of those who practiced magic brought their books together and began burning them in the sight of all; and they counted up the price of them and found it fifty thousand pieces of silver."*

Silversmiths who crafted images of Artemis worried about their financial loss resulting from Paul's ministry in Ephesus. Many were turning to Christ from idolatry. The silversmiths created an uproar at the theatre (Acts 19:23-29). An inscription discovered at the theatre in Ephesus informs us that a silver image of Artemis and other images were displayed at the theatre during civic meetings there. [187] A monument discovered in 1984 near the theatre confirms Luke's recording of both silversmiths and temple wardens of Artemis in Ephesus during the first century.[188]

In Acts 19:31 Paul was urged by some Asiarchs of Ephesus not to enter the local theatre where a hostile demonstration against him was occurring over the worship of Artemis. Many scholars in the late nineteenth century declared this report of a riot in Ephesus was a fabrication. However, *"it has now been shown that no less than 18 historical references or terms that occur in Acts 19:23-40 have been verified by archaeological inscriptions."* [189] These include: "Temple of the Great goddess Artemis"; "temple guardian"; 'fallen from heaven"; "town clerk"; "standing courts"; and "proconsul."[190]

Some express skepticism of Luke's use of the word Asiarchs but Strabo writing in the first century mentioned Asiarchs from Ephesus confirming that Luke had correctly identified these locally appointed political officials. [191] Strabo mentioned that some of the well to do *"men hold the chief places in the province , being called Asiarchs."*[192] That these men were called friends of Paul informs us that Paul's ministry was not merely among the poor, and that the educated and wealthy were not as opposed to Paul as were the superstitious. Over a dozen inscriptions have now been found confirming Luke's use of Asiarchs.[193]

Also mentioned is the chief executive magistrate of Roman era Ephesus, the *"town clerk."* This person kept records, had oversight of temple money etc. and was directly accountable to Rome. Some of the past town clerks even appear on coins of Ephesus because of their great influence. In addition, there were proconsuls and a Roman district court in Ephesus (Acts 19:35-41). In Ephesus, 1st century statues of Artemis have been found.[194] Luke was proven accurate on each point.

The book of Philemon deals with a runaway slave the Apostle Paul won to Christ and then sent him back to Philemon, his owner requesting that he be forgiven and treated like a Christian brother rather than a slave. An interesting inscription erected by a freed slave in Laodicea was dedicated to Marcus Sestius Philemon. Though we cannot verify that this is the same Philemon, it may be more than coincidence that this is from the same area, and both concern freeing a slave.[195]

There were many advantages in every area of life from being a Roman citizen, and it was a much sought after privilege. Citizens were treated better than imperial subjects who did not possess citizenship. These included traveling freely throughout the empire. One could not be flogged or detained without first being tried in court. They had the right to appeal a decision and magistrates or governors could not block appeals. Paul employed his privileges in Jerusalem after his rescue from an irate Jewish mob, and when Festus held him in prison to please the Jews (Acts 22:23-29; 25:7-12; 26:32).[196]

Paul was born a citizen, which informs us that his parents were citizens. There were several other ways one could become a Roman citizen. These include being rewarded for completion of military service or for having performed some exceptional service for the state or for a government official. There was also the opportunity to purchase citizenship through money, supplies or products. The Roman commander states he became a citizen though purchasing it (Acts 22:28). Citizens had documents proving their citizenship which they carried with them when traveling.[197]

After Paul was arrested in Jerusalem, he was taken to Caesarea to escape those who has sworn to kill him (Acts 23:24-26). He was under the protection there of Antonius Felix. Josephus, Tacitus, and Suetonius trace the career of Felix (52-60 A.D.) from his rise to the circumstances of his replacement by Festus. Only Josephus refers to Festus' term as procurator of Judea. None of this information refers to their relationship with Paul but confirms the rule of Felix who was then followed by Festus.[198]

The Antonia Fortress in Jerusalem was just south of the pool of Bethesda and was connected by two bridges to the northern side of the temple Mount. Herod rebuilt this tower and named it after Mark Antony. This became the Roman Garrison in Jerusalem. It is referred to numerous times as the barracks in reference to Paul's troubles with the Jews during his last visit to Jerusalem. This is where the tribune Claudius Lysias and the Roman soldiers took Paul (Acts 21:34, 37; 23:24).

The Antonia fortress was destroyed in 70 A.D. but rebuilt around 135 A.D, during the time of Emperor Hadrian. It is a popular misconception that the Praetorium, the Roman governor's residence, was at the Antonia Fortress though it was not.[199]

In Beirut, known as Berytus in ancient times, excavations found many buildings from the Roman era. Also found was a Latin inscription mentioning Agrippa II and Bernice who were mentioned by Luke. (Acts 25:13).[200]

Paul mentions that the entire praetorian guard had heard the Gospel because of his imprisonment in Rome (Phi. 1:13). This special category of troops was established by Caesar Augustus. The main duty of these soldiers was to guard the emperor and his family. They were also assigned to other duties within Rome such as policing the games as well as confining criminals.[201]

Paul's associate Titus is told of Paul's intention to spend the winter (probably 64 A.D.) in Nicopolis which was in northwestern Greece (Titus 3:12). Subscriptions on some ancient manuscripts of 1Timothy and Titus indicate that Paul wrote those two letters from Nicopolis, which is very possible. Strabo mentioned there were two harbors at Nicopolis. [202] Paul frequently stayed at harbor cities as strategic for ministry and the ease of transportation and communication.

At the southern entrance of the Roman forum is the Arch of Titus. The arch depicts the destruction of the Jerusalem temple by Roman general Titus in 70 A.D. This was a fulfillment of Jesus' prediction nearly forty years earlier.[203] *"Following the destruction of Jerusalem and the burning of the temple, for twenty-five years the Emperors Vespasian, Titus and Domitian issued a series of coins to commemorate the victory over the Jews in denominations of bronze, silver and gold."*[204]

During construction work at the Megiddo prison (Israel) in 2005 archaeological remains were discovered. They were remains of a third century church with a beautiful large mosaic. There were three inscriptions in the mosaic. The third inscription read *"The God-loving Akeptous has offered the table to God Jesus Christ as a memorial."*[205] Coins from the emperors reigning from 218-305 A.D. were also found. Absence of later coins meant the building had been abandoned quite early in the fourth century.

This discovery provides several insights as it seems reasonable to date the end of the building's usage within the first decade of the fourth century or slightly before. The contributions are the acknowledgment of Jesus as God, and the use of the communion table in early Christian celebration.[206]

The book of Revelation is quite an enigma to most readers, but archaeology can enlighten us on the historical context just as it does for other books of the Bible.

John is on Patmos, a Greek island "for the word of God and for the testimony of Jesus Christ." Though John does not clarify what he means, scholars assume he has been banished there by Rome because of his ministry and refusal to acknowledge that Caesar is Lord. This is assumed because the Roman historian Tacitus, in the beginning of the second century mentions Romans exiling political prisoners to three other islands in the Aegean. These Islands of exile were Donousa, Gyaros, and Amorgos.[207]

Evidence indicates continual occupation of Patmos, so it was not a deserted island nor only exiting as a penal colony for Rome. Ancient writers give no evidence of mines or quarries on the island. It is possible John was involved in missionary activity, though it is assumed he would have chosen a more populous area for evangelism if he had a choice.[208]

Smyrna was an ancient city in the Roman province of Asia Minor, which during the Roman era became a wealthy port city. There were religious temples in Smyrna for many gods and for the emperors. This was the first city in Asia Minor to host the cult of emperor worship. The strong emphasis on emperor worship in Smyrna no doubt accounts for the severity of persecution mentioned concerning this church (Rev. 2:8-11).[209] The church there must have originated from the Apostle Paul's long ministry in nearby Ephesus.

In the first century, Pergamum was the second most important city of the Roman Province of Asia. Inscriptions and artwork found indicate there was a community of Jews in Pergamum since at least the first century B.C. There were also temples and shrines to many gods as well as for emperor worship.[210]

Thyatira has yielded little at this point in regard to the first century. Inscriptions found indicate there were many types of commerce and many gods worshipped at Thyatira. A much cheaper source of purple dye was available locally which made it a very profitable trade. Acts 16:14 mentions Lydia who sold purple fabrics had moved from Thyatira to Philippi. An inscription honoring a purple-dye dealer from Thyatira was found in Philippi, indicating such moves for commercial purposes did occur.[211]

One of the seven churches of Revelation was that of Sardis (Rev. 3:2-5). Excavations there revealed a temple of Artemis whom the Romans called Diana. The Bible uses the name Diana. The worship of Diana from at least 550 B.C. continued until the impact of the Gospel and churches resulted in the abandonment of her temple in Sardis. Jesus gave the most severe rebuke of all the churches to Sardis for its compromise with paganism (Rev. 3:1).

The warnings (3:2-3) "Wake up" and "you will not know at what hour I will come upon you" make sense in light of the history of Sardis. Twice the city had been captured by enemies because of a lack of vigilance, "(*Cyrus in 549 BC and Antiochus III in 195 BC) ... In both cases the wall to the city was breached while the city slept.*"[212]

Also, Sardis had been hit in a twelve-year span (17-29 A.D.) by four sudden earthquakes. The quake in 17 A.D. destroyed most of the city.[213] There was also a major quake in 60 A.D. that destroyed much of Sardis while the people slept. They had apparently ignored the tremors that had preceded it. Emperor Tiberius granted a large sum of money and a tax exemption of five years to enable rebuilding the city.[214] The awareness of the suddenness and inability to defend the city from the earthquakes would make Jesus' warnings especially urgent to this church.

One of the promises given to this church was that the overcomer would not have their name blotted out of the book of life (3:5). In Greek cities, citizens names were in the public registry. The names of those convicted of crime were blotted out.[215]

The church at Sardis apparently responded to Jesus' warnings and promises, as the evidence of a sizable Christian community has been found continuing there into the fifth and sixth centuries A.D. This includes the excavation of a small church behind the temple of Diana dating to about the fifth century.[216]

The only church in Revelation 2-3 that is not criticized for any failures or shortcomings is that of Philadelphia. Excavations to this point indicate that there was apparently no official imperial cult presence or important pagan temples in Philadelphia during the 1st century. This may have prevented problems of syncretism that were extensive in the other churches listed[217] as well as accounting for the "open door" which may suggest greater opportunity for Christian witness there. Excavation has been very limited because a modern city covers the site.

With the Roman takeover of the entire region in 133 B.C., the main trade route was redirected through Asia Minor making Laodicea the location of a major crossroad. By the 1st century B.C., it was one of the richest and most prominent cities in the Province of Asia (Rev. 3:17). Unfortunately, it was also a center of pagan temples, altars and statues of many supposed gods and goddesses. Many of these alleged deities were depicted on first century coins of Laodicea. There was also an imperial temple by around 81 A.D.

This entire region has been subjected to recurring and serious earthquakes. Following the serious destruction of Laodicea in 60 A.D., the city rebuilt without any outside imperial assistance. This exemplified the proud, self-sufficient attitude mentioned in revelation. "I am rich, and have become wealthy and have need of nothing" (3:17).

Laodicea also had a medical school with advanced knowledge of anatomy and especially famous for its eye salve which was mentioned by ancient sources including Strabo (see Rev. 3:18).[218] The city was also famous for its black wool and dyed wool, which would have been seen as an obvious contrast with the statement about believers clothing themselves with righteousness of Christ (white garments) (Rev. 3:18).

Unlike Hierapolis with its hot mineral springs, or Colossae with its cold mountain water, Laodicea had to pipe its water in from nearly 5 miles away. Jesus was not saying He preferred a cold church. The church is being condemned for providing neither spiritual refreshment (the cold water) nor spiritual healing (hot mineral water). This water though saturated with minerals, became lukewarm while being pumped to Laodicea.[219]

This is the historical basis for Jesus words, "*I know your deeds, that you are neither cold nor hot; I would that you were cold or hot. So, because you are lukewarm, and neither hot nor cold, I will spit you out of my mouth.*" (Rev. 3:15-16). Expensive fines were threatened for anyone attempting to divert the water, use it for irrigation or intentionally damage a water pipe, indicating the water was necessary and highly valued despite the taste.[220]

Patmos is a 13 square mile volcanic island about 60 miles southwest of Ephesus off the coast of Asia Minor (Turkey). The Romans often used remote islands at which to exile undesirables. John had been determined to be one of those persons through his teaching and church leadership. He is thought to have been exiled there during the reign of Domitian in 94 A.D. Romans frequently tortured individuals prior to exiling them, so John, though elderly, may have experienced torture. Patmos during the 1st century was not an uninhabited prison colony, but had a town, harbor, stadium, and a few pagan temples.[221]

Pisidian Antioch in the province of Galatia was the site of a sermon by Paul in the synagogue that brought out nearly the whole city the following week (Acts 13:14-44). Extensive research has resulted in discovering many Christian inscriptions in the area indicated the strong impact Paul and Barnabas had. A first century church and two fifth century churches have been found there.[222]

Thessalonica was about 95 miles west of Philippi, in the province of Macedonia, Greece. Luke wrote in Acts that the Jews had some local Christians brought before the city officials called politarchs. Skeptics rejected this designation of city officials as an error until inscriptions were found, including on the wall near the city gate referring to these leaders. We now know there were multiple politarchs, usually five, during the Roman period.[223] The inscription on the city wall begins "In the time of the Politarchs ..."[224]

"Further, one of the politarchs mentioned on an inscription from Thessalonica was Secundus, which is the same Latin name as one of the Christians from Thessalonica (Acts 20:4).[225] Though it is possible these are the same person it is uncertain. Another 1st century inscription mentions a politarch named Aristarchus which matches another name of a Christian friend of Paul's from Thessalonica. (Acts 19:29, 27:2).[226] Again, we do not know if these were the same person, but they prove to be valid names of the locale and era, further substantiating Luke's reliability as an historian.

Paul arrived in Athens after the disturbances in Berea and was awaiting Silas and Timothy (Acts 17:17). Paul was appalled at the multitude of idols in the city. The Roman satirist Juvenal remarked it was easier in Athens to find a god than a man. Paul even found an alter dedicated to an 'unknown god which he used as the springboard for his preaching' (Acts 17:21).

Others have mentioned the discovery of altars to unknown gods in Athens. Apollonius of Tyana, who died in 98 A.D. said of Athens as *"where alters are set up in honor even of unknown gods."* [227] Pausanias visited Athens between 143-159 A.D. and mentioned, *"The temple of Athene Skiras is also here, and one of Zeus further off, and altars of the 'Unknown gods.'"* [228] When Paul gave his sermon in Athens, he quoted a Greek poet's words, *"For we are indeed his offspring"* (Acts 17:28). This is from the poet Aratus writing in the 3rd century B.C. Aratus also speaks of God as one. [229]

Luke accurately assessed those in the marketplace Paul sought to convince. He wrote that *"the Athenians and strangers visiting there used to spend their time in nothing other than telling or hearing something new"* (Acts 17:21). The pagan writers Demosthenes, Thucydides and others gave the same assessment of the Athenians. [230]

The term used as an insult of Paul in Athens is translated 'idle babbler' in Acts 17:18. The Greek word 'spermologos' literally means seed picker. This word choice shows Luke's knowledge of Stoic culture and language. This was the precise word used by the founder of Stoicism, Zeno of Citium to insult a follower. [231]

When Paul was to be sent to the emperor, he was placed under the charge of Julius a centurion of the Augustan cohort. First century inscriptions inform us that the Augustan cohort functioned primarily in Syria, but were also stationed in Galilee and Judea which was part of the province of Syria. [232] While awaiting trial in Rome Paul declares that the entire praetorian guard has heard the gospel because of his imprisonment (Phil. 1:13). From Roman history we know that prisoners from the provinces brought to Rome were placed under the control of the praetorian guard. [233]

Manuscript Evidence of the New Testament

There are some skeptics, who dismiss the value of the manuscripts as evidence for the authenticity of the Christian faith. One reason for such denials is that the early manuscripts disprove the late dates the skeptics want to assign to the biblical documents in order to discredit the writings.

The reason that the manuscripts are so important is that, we have some manuscripts so much closer to the events and relationships they describe than those for any other ancient writing. This proximity to the events lends great credibility to the content and descriptions in those narratives. A second reason the manuscripts are so valuable is that we have so many as well as such early ones, that they can be compared and analyzed to assure that we have a reliable text of our present New Testament.

We have over 5,800 Greek New Testament manuscripts, fragments, or complete copies, 10,000 Latin manuscripts and 9,300 in other ancient languages. The earliest of these is apparently the John Rylands Library Papyrus P52. It is written in Greek and consists of the gospel of John 18:31-33 on one side and of verses 18:37-38 on the reverse. This fragment is dated approximately A.D. 125.[234]

That indicates we have a fragment of John that dates from between approximately 55 and 85 years from the writing of the original! That proximity to the original writing is unheard of in regard to ancient writings! Discovered in Egypt, the fragment reveals how distant the written words of John were being copied or disseminated in the early second century A.D. It being in Egypt in the first quarter of the 2nd century also brings into question whether John may not have been the latest biblical Gospel written as has been usually assumed.[235]

The Chester Beatty papyri, parts of which were purchased originally by him and other segments by the University of Michigan contain fragments of the Gospels, Acts and almost the entirety of Paul's letters. This collection of manuscripts is dated at about 200 A.D.[236]

Codex Sinaiticus is the oldest manuscript found so far of the complete New Testament. It is from the fourth century A.D. It was discovered in 1844 at St. Catherine's Monastery at Mt. Sinai.

Perhaps you have wondered how it is possible to obtain reliable dates for the writing of ancient manuscripts. Are the dates given complete guesswork or are they based on the preferred date of those who discover or study the documents? It does happen that scholars will sometimes give a date that they prefer for a document in order to justify their prior assumptions. An example was skeptical scholars declaring that the Gospel of John was not written until about 150 A.D.

While there is usually an approximate rather than an exact date for ancient writings, the dates are not normally based upon mere guesswork or preferences of the discoverer or other scholars. Paleography is the study of ancient and pre-modern writings in scrolls, manuscripts, hand written books (codices), and that study establishes the basis for dating the document.

Those involved in this study have a variety of clues to help them obtain a reliable approximation for the date the document in question was written. Clues include the style of writing, the spelling of certain words and language itself which changes over time. Other clues can be the type of ink used, comparison with other known writings, the level of excavation at which the document was found and other artifacts found with the document, such as coins, pottery, type of weapons, etc.

Another skeptical method in attempting to discredit the manuscript evidence is the criticism of variant readings in the New Testament manuscripts. If a different word or spelling occurs in a manuscript from another manuscript, that is considered a variant reading or a discrepancy. If a different word is substituted in one manuscript at the same place it is an occurrence that needs to be resolved. However, if that exact same variation occurs in the exact same place in 200 different manuscripts, the skeptics claim that as 200 variants.

This enables them to greatly exaggerate the actual number of variations in the texts far beyond reality. This is a dishonest method of creating the illusion that the New Testament text is completely unreliable and unknowable.

In reality, uncertainty as to the text only occurs in half a dozen cases for the entire New Testament. In none of those cases is a major or significant teaching of the Christian faith involved. Therefore, contrary to the claims and pretenses of skeptics, we know that we have a reliable New Testament text.

Attacking the Truth of the Gospels

Many different approaches have been used by atheists, skeptics, Liberal theologians, and other non-Christian critics in order to avoid the authenticity and validity of the Biblical Gospel's witness to Jesus Christ. Such persons are always looking for excuses to discount or dismiss the evidence these Gospels provide concerning who Jesus really is and what He has said, done and can do.

The Biblical Gospels are not rejected due to lack of credibility or evidence of their reliability but due to anti-supernatural and anti-Christian bias. Contrary to all the explanations and assertions these skeptical critics make regarding the Gospels, the actual reason they reject these documents is because they speak of an all-powerful God to whom we are accountable and include miracles.

Each of the various evasive arguments these skeptics assert is presented as the genuine truth about the Gospels in books, journals, news magazines, on TV, and the internet. This flood of disinformation (in earlier generations they would have been called deception or lies) makes it essential to understand and see through the presented pretenses.

The first necessity is to remind people that assertions and declarations are not the same as evidence and proof. Anything can be asserted by anyone. My own statements that the Bible is authentic and reliable are merely unproven assertions until I present evidence and argument that gives a basis for believing my statements to be true.[237] Most of the criticisms of the Bible are merely assertions that have not and cannot be validated by any evidence.

Books such as Thomas Paine's, The Age of Reason, the writings of John Shelby Spong, and novels by Dan Brown are filled with critical and misleading assertions without evidence. These assertions are cleverly presented as if they are facts that discredit the Bible. It is incredible that merely asserting something to be true, without evidence can apparently influence large numbers of people.

Paine assumed the only genuine evidence of God was the physical creation and that any claim to special revelation or written revelation from God was false. The following statement is the foundation upon which Paine bases his many assumptions and assertions:

"It is a contradiction in terms and ideas, to call anything a revelation that comes to us second-hand either verbally or in writing. Revelation is necessarily limited to the first communication – after this, it is only an account of something which that person says was a revelation made to him; and though he may find himself obliged to believe it, it cannot be incumbent on me to believe it in the same manner; for it was not a revelation made to me, and I have only his word for it that it was made to him."[238]

Paine has made several assumptions in this declaration that may not be obvious to the reader. First, he has arbitrarily declared what can or cannot be revelation. Second, he has assumed that though there is a God, he is not interested, able, or willing to communicate with humans. Third, he has assumed that there is no such individual as a specifically chosen messenger from God or a genuine prophet. Fourth, he has assumed that no alleged revelation or communication from God has had accompanying evidence that would confirm or verify it to be of supernatural origin. Fifth, Paine has assumed that no apparent revelation would be incumbent upon him or anyone else unless made directly from God to that individual. Sixth, he has assumed that he knows God would not communicate with us, without any means for him to know that about God. There is no way for him to know that because he has assumed there is no knowledge of God beyond the creation.

Not only did Paine not prove any of these assumptions he made no attempt to do so. We are to disbelieve what is said to be divine revelation because it is supposedly just someone saying so, but we are to believe what Paine has written without evidence because he says so.

John Shelby Spong, was a twentieth century Episcopal priest who had been defrocked for heresy. He claimed that the apostle Paul never taught the physical resurrection of Christ. It is obvious that the physical resurrection of Christ is assumed in many passages but in 1Corinthians 15 after emphasizing that Christ has risen from the dead Paul gets very specific: *"So also is the resurrection of the dead. It is sown a perishable body, it is raised an imperishable body; ... it is sown a natural body, it is raised a spiritual body."* (15:42, 44).

Some skeptics such as Spong claim it was a spiritual resurrection not a physical, bodily resurrection of the corpse. The response to such skeptics of the physical resurrection has been to ask, *"What dies? The body! Then what must be brought back to life?"* Without a physical, bodily resurrection, Jesus' body would have been found in the tomb. No one would have believed in a resurrection if the body was still dead. It is obvious the entire New Testament teaches the literal, physical resurrection of Christ.

Which Gospel Was the First Written?

Most modern scholars consider Mark to have been the first of the four canonical Gospels to have been written. The skeptical scholars also assume that Mark was dependent upon a mysterious writing they designate as Q. This has never been found because it does not exist. Mark's dependence is thought to have been primarily upon Peter (and probably Barnabas who discipled Mark). A major reason for the assumption that Mark was first is that the skeptics assume Matthew and Luke drew much of their information from Mark. In other words, they assume Matthew and Luke are dependent upon Mark.

There are various arguments proposed for this dependence upon Mark. One is that about 93% of Mark's material is included in Matthew and Luke. Another argument is that Mark's sequence seems to be the original. When Matthew's sequence varies from Mark, Luke's agrees with Mark. But when Luke's sequence varies from Mark, Matthew agrees with Mark. Mark also seems more primitive, in comparison with the other Gospels. [239] For example, he does not include much of the actual teaching of Jesus but usually merely mentions that Jesus taught.

The early church, however, much closer to the entire situation, generally accepted that Matthew was the first written. Mark may have written a more abbreviated account for an unknown reason. Also since Matthew was an eyewitness, it is not likely he relied upon Mark who apparently was not an eye witness. Mark 6:45-8:26 is a very significant section, yet Luke does not include it. Matthew and Luke also agree in sections where Mark has something else.

The evidence suggests that Matthew certainly was not dependent upon Mark. In fact, Matthew and Mark may have been completely unfamiliar with each other's writings. Matthew was writing from personal memory and experience.[240] Luke wrote from extensive research which might have included Mark's Gospel. The Scholars generally ignore or discount Jesus' explanations of the Holy Spirit's bringing to the disciples' memories all he taught them (John 14:6, 16:13-14).

Claims the Gospel Texts Have Been Altered

Another attack on the New Testament is that the text has been altered over the centuries during the hand copying and we have no genuine idea of the original contents of these writings and no reliable information about Jesus. This attack fails for at least three reasons.

First, to know the Biblical text had been altered they would need to know the original text which, in their attack they have admitted they do not know. It would be necessary to know the original text to know changes had been made in it. In other words, they would need manuscripts that show alterations between them to prove such changes were made. No such manuscripts exist. The skeptics have merely assumed and asserted what they want to be true instead of showing that those assumptions are true.

Our English Old Testament is translated from the Hebrew text. It is important to be aware that, many of our quotes and references to the Old Testament in the New Testament are from the Septuagint (Greek) translation rather than from the Hebrew. Also, New Testament writers often paraphrase an Old Testament reference rather than quoting it exactly. This has sometimes created the illusion of contradictions between the Old Testament and New Testament texts.[241]

Secondly, there is no evidence of any significant alterations in the text. The manuscripts do sometimes show variations in pronouns, misspellings, and there are a few minor

68

additions to the text called interpolations. These variations do not involve any major or significant teaching of the New Testament. These mistakes and minor additions are now well known and either identified or eliminated in the modern English New Testament translations.

These interpolations or additions to the text were made in ancient times in an attempt to explain something in the original text or to conform one account more closely to another (which ignored the different context and purpose of the different accounts). Critics have magnified these insignificant additions way out of proportion to their significance. They do not affect any authentic teaching of the New Testament and their removal does not in any way alter the message or meaning of the text. However, some conservatives worry that these corrections of the text are attempts to eliminate or alter biblical teaching.

Thirdly, we now have over 5,000 ancient manuscripts and fragments of the New Testament, which have enabled us to not only eliminate the additions to the text but also to know that we have a reliable and authentic text in all essentials. The science of textual criticism (comparing the ancient manuscripts, ancient quotes in other writings and ancient translations) enables us to determine the correct reading of the vast majority of the original text. There are also ancient lectionaries, which are selections of biblical text that were copied to be read in the worship services of the early churches.

As theologian and philosopher J.P. Moreland has written, *"Besides this, virtually the entire New Testament could be reproduced from citations contained in the works of the early church Fathers. There are some thirty-two thousand citations in the writings of the fathers prior to the council of Nicaea (325)."*[242] From the comparison of these sources, over 98% of the New Testament text, is known to be accurate.

There are not more than twenty uncertainties in the entire New Testament, only half a dozen of which are significant and none of those involves a major teaching of the Christian Faith. Some skeptics try to make the number of problems seem immense by emphasizing that the exact same variant reading in the same location in one hundred manuscripts is one hundred discrepancies instead of the one variant it actually is.

Is the Jesus of History The Christ of Faith?

One of the attacks on the Gospels asserts that the Jesus of history is not the same as the Christ of faith. Skeptic Kenneth C. Davis wrote, "*since the nineteenth century—and especially in recent years—it has become popular to distinguish between the Jesus of 'faith' as presented in the New Testament, and the 'historical Jesus.'*" He goes on to discredit the New Testament as 'hearsay evidence.'

Another skeptic, John Crossan makes the distinction that what is meant by essential when applied to Jesus depends upon "*whether we are talking about the canonical or the historical Jesus.*"[243] He declares that he is going for the historical truth about Jesus. He mentions that he will not simply pick out the best known of Jesus' sayings but "*I present instead those sayings that, in my best historical judgment are original with Jesus.*" His 'best historical judgment' does not appear to be very good as we will see. Crossan goes on to disparage the canonical Gospels which he mentions as written forty to sixty years after Jesus' death.

Instead of the biblical documents he prefers to quote the "Gospel of Thomas" which was written another twenty-five to fifty or more years after the canonical Gospels.[244] Thomas also has obvious Gnostic characteristics. Next, Crossan relates the imaginary "Q" document with verses from the Gospels of Matthew and Luke. Presuming information to have been included in legitimate Gospels from an assumed writing that has never been found nor proven to have existed, informs us of the actual "historical" basis of Crossan's writing. Assertions based upon assumptions and imagination translate in the minds of such skeptics into reliable history.

What is popular is seldom what is actually important or true. The assertion that the Jesus of history is not the same as the Christ of faith means that the Christ believed in by Christians for the past 2,000 years is not the same as the Jesus who actually lived back in the first century. This assumes that the Gospels were altered over time to present a supernatural Jesus though he was only a man who was an effective teacher and great moral example for us.

Of course, because these skeptics reject the testimony of the Gospels, there is no way for them to genuinely know much of anything about Jesus (except for the few references in the

Talmad and secular writers). How would they know he was an effective teacher or great moral example? When they reject the validity of the biblical documents there is no basis for knowing much of anything about Jesus apart from the few non-biblical references to Jesus mentioned previously. Such writers choose what they like depending upon the particular alteration of Jesus they promote.

German theologian Leonhard Goppelt rejects the pessimism of Bultmann and most German theologians. Goppelt *"held that the 'Christ of faith' must be found by searching for, not separating from, the 'Christ of History.'"*[245]

It is true that there are a few references to Jesus by several early historians and other writers, as well as in the Jewish Talmud. These statements confirm a few major details about Jesus and the early Church. Most critics ignore those early sources and take some information from the Gospels that they like or prefer and reject whatever contradicts their own thinking. Others show a preference for the Gnostic gospels written from 50 to 300 years after the biblical Gospels.

There is absolutely no textual or historical evidence of changes having been made in the presentations of Jesus Christ in the Gospels. The most reasonable conclusion to make from this lack of evidence to the contrary is therefore, that the Jesus of History and the Christ of faith are the same person. It is further obvious that assertions to the effect they are not the same merely reflect the preferences of those making such claims. They prefer their own unbelieving speculations rather than the reliable documents we actually possess.

Claims of Very Late Dates of Composition

Another of the older attacks on the credibility of the Gospels was to date them as late as the middle of the second century A.D. or even later, and then claim that we had no idea who the writers actually were nor of the validity of the content of the documents. Note there is series of assumption here. First the critics declare the writings were of late date which is contrary to the evidence. Then upon that assumption they claim that the writings could not be by the persons historically attributed to be the writers.

They further assume from those prior assumptions that since we did not have eyewitness and first-hand reports, we could therefore not know whether any of the information was authentic. They follow this up with the conclusion that therefore none of the writings should be accepted as valid or true. This attack on the credibility of the Gospels has become thoroughly discredited through growing knowledge of first century Israel and through more objective study of the entire New Testament including the Gospels.

J.A.T. Robinson, was a scholar in the Liberal theological camp which generally seeks to eliminate confidence in the validity of the Biblical documents. In his textbook, Redating the New Testament, Robinson pointed out that there is no mention in any of the New Testament of the actual destruction of Jerusalem in 70 A.D. and of the end of institutional Judaism. He wrote that this absence is very strong evidence the entire New Testament had to have been written prior to 70 A.D. The book of Revelation might possibly be an exception.

Robinson said it would be incredible that no mention of these events would be in the New Testament if some of it was written later, when such facts would have been strong support for the argument that the Christian Faith had now replaced Judaism as God's vehicle in the world. The fact that Jesus had specifically predicted the destruction of the temple in Jerusalem prior to his execution would have made this a very telling argument in support of such a conclusion (Luke 19:28, 41-44; 21:5-6, 20-24).

This places the entire New Testament (possibly excepting Revelation) within less than forty years of the recorded events. Another scholar has said that references to the murder of Steven and execution of James would seem to indicate that the absence of any reference to the executions of Paul and Peter in the mid 60's as additional evidence that the New Testament must have been written even prior to that. This would place the New Testament documents within thirty-five years or less of the events they present. Either of these dates are easily within the generation of the Apostles and many of the original believers.

There is no longer any reason to doubt that the Gospels of Matthew and John were eyewitness accounts. Nor is there justification for rejecting Luke's account as the result of careful research and earlier ministry involvement with the Apostle Paul. Mark is also known from Biblical accounts and ministered with Barnabas, Peter, and Paul, so he too had access to firsthand information, if he was not in actuality an eyewitness.

It is no longer tenable to assume that any of the New Testament documents were written later then the early second half of the first century A.D. This makes them authentic and credible documents of the life of Jesus and the early Church.

Tied to this early dating for the Gospels is the evidence from the earliest manuscripts discovered so far for each Gospel. Some of these early manuscripts are of more than one Gospel. These document dates are all from archaeologist Titus Kennedy's Excavating the Evidence for Jesus.[246]

For Matthew: P03 & P104 date between 100-200 A.D.; P64 & P67 date between 150-200 A.D.; P77 dates between 150-200 A.D.; P1 and P45 date between 200-250 A.D.

For Mark: P137 dates between 100-200 A.D.; P45 dates between 200-250 A.D.

For Luke: P4 dates between 150-200 A.D.; P75 dates from 175-225 A.D.; P45 and P111 date from 200-250 A.D.

For John: P52 from 90-175 A.D.; P66 and P90 from 100-200 A.D.; P75 from 175-225 A.D.; P5, P22, P45, and P119 date from 200-250 A.D.

Claims the Gospels Reflect the Issues of the Early Church

A third effort to devalue and defeat the testimony of the Gospels is the claim that they reflect the concerns and issues of the early church rather than historically valid, original information about Jesus. For anyone who actually reads the New Testament without a jaundiced attitude, it is evident that it is in the New Testament Letters that the Apostles are focused upon the problems of the early church, not the Gospels. The time frame the Gospels deal with is prior to the origin of the church and there is not the slightest indication of the intrusion of church problems into the Gospels.

Claims the Gospels Reveal the Church's Understanding Rather Than Genuine History

Another type of attack is the claim that the New Testament Gospels record the early church's understanding of Jesus rather than providing any real factual knowledge of Jesus or of the disciple's experience of Jesus. The Gospels do, of course, reflect the original understanding of Jesus from His apostles' experiences with Him. But this criticism like others, assumes that the miracles and statements attributed to Jesus were later additions.

This criticism also assumes that the church created the New Testament instead of the New Testament creating the church. It is the oral teachings of the apostles incorporated in the New Testament that the church had its inception. The criticism also assumes deception on the part of the actual writers of the Gospels who present the information as if they were either with Jesus or obtained first-hand knowledge of Jesus from those who were with him.

These claims also assume that critics writing twenty centuries later are better judges of the authenticity and origin of the writings than the first century recipients of those writings. Again, there is no evidence of such changes in any of the Gospel manuscripts.

Claims That People In Ancient Times Were Susceptible to Miracle Stories

It is claimed that people in pre-scientific times were superstitious, more gullible, and therefore they were susceptible to believe miracle stories. It is true that there have often been miracles asserted to have happened without any evidence or reason to believe them. There have also been many cases of faked miracles past and present. Though false miracles have been asserted and assumed, that argument does not eliminate justification for accepting the miracles ascribed to Jesus to be genuine for several reasons.

First, there were eyewitnesses of the reported miracles, including Jesus' opponents, not only his followers. Secondly, also even ancient people knew that someone born blind did not suddenly gain the ability to see; that a person with a withered arm did not receive restoration of the arm just because someone made a statement to that effect. These were not fakable events.

Even in the first century everyone knew that dead men did not suddenly come back to life. None of these events would have been believed by the people in first century Israel unless there was incontrovertible proof they had occurred. It is important to recall that these were not examples of persons arriving from far away who claimed these events had happened to them. These miracles were performed on people known to the local populace and many local people were actual witnesses of the transforming events.

The claims that first century people were more gullible and easier to convince of supernatural events has been greatly exaggerated. In fact, it seems a good case could be made that current generations are no less gullible than those in the ancient past.

Huge crowds give credence to claims of various faith healers. There are numerous mediums claiming to contact the dead and give advice in return for a fee. Many visit sites where someone has claimed to have had a vision of the virgin Mary. Millions worship the latest music sensation. There are even those who follow those who claim to be the return of Jesus. This is though none of those claimants arrived in the way Jesus declared he would return, and none of them give any evidence that would validate their claim. Consider the multitudes who believe urban legends and various conspiracy theories.

Claims that the Four Gospels Were Chosen Because They Portray A Supernatural Jesus

In some recent books asserting to present historical facts, it has been claimed that the canonical Gospels were chosen from among dozens of competing Gospels because these four portrayed a supernatural Jesus. Such claims are, however, fraudulent for several reasons. As an aside, this is an interesting argument because many skeptics also claim that the first three Gospels in the New Testament do not portray Jesus as divine.

The first reason to reject such claims is that most of the other alleged Gospels also portray Jesus as supernatural and present a fantastical portrayal of events. Secondly, the supposedly competing Gospels were not written until after the close of the New Testament canon. The so-called Gnostic Gospels were written too late to be considered as part of the inspired documents. They were written in the second, third and fourth centuries A.D. whereas the authentic Gospels were written in the first century no later than 70 A.D.[247]

Third, many these later 'gospels', falsely claimed to be written by apostles and others who had been dead long before these narratives were written. Fourthly, these alleged gospels were not hidden by the church as asserted by some recent authors. Instead, they were rejected because of teachings that conflicted with the known teachings of Jesus' apostles as well as for the reasons listed above. Finally, many of these gospels include fantastic and superstitious exaggerations of reality.

As Philip Jenkins wrote, *"Since the Gnostics had little regard for objective historical truth, their retellings of the story of Jesus claimed not a particle of historical authenticity."*[248]

Jenkins also stated that *"Gnostics wanted a Jesus who said certain things, and they wrote documents asserting that he had done so. Accordingly, the Gnostics neatly foreshadowed postmodern attitudes toward subjectivity."*[249] In other words, much like the Gnostics, some modern scholars create a Jesus more in agreement with their subjective bias than the actual historical Jesus.

Read these alleged gospels rather than the exaggerated claims made about them by their advocates, and if you also read the authentic Gospels, you can readily see the difference in quality and believability between them and the counterfeit substitutes some skeptics prefer. As Jenkins adds, *"Though contemporary writers use the Gnostic gospels to portray alternative models of Christianity, we see that these rival movements were much later historically than their orthodox counterparts, and were actually formulated in reaction against a preexisting orthodoxy, so they cannot claim to represent equally valid or ancient views of Jesus."*[250]

Claims that the Miracles Were Later Additions to the Gospels

The basis for the rejection of the authenticity and validity of the biblical Gospels is because they include God and the supernatural. This excuse to escape the genuineness of the Biblical Gospels asserts that the miracles are legends added later to the Gospels. These alleged additions are said to have been made to elevate Jesus to deity as His reputation grew in the minds of His followers.

However, legendary development around a dead leader takes a long time to develop. The Biblical documents were written too close to the actual events they disclose for legends to have developed. Also, there is no evidence of such accretions to the Biblical writings. There are no biblical manuscripts that lack the miracles. In addition, the critics would need to know the original text to know that the miracles were added later, which they admit they do not know. The Biblical miracles are completely integrated into their contexts, flow naturally with the accounts, and fit with the personality and character of Jesus.

Attempting to remove the miracles creates discontinuities and incoherence in the biblical text. Whereas, adding miracles into accounts of other famous persons, the supposed miracles reveal themselves to be legendary. The added miracles do not fit into the context and character of those persons lives. The rejection of the miracles of the Bible are not because they lack credibility but because of anti-supernatural and anti-Christian bias. The miracles were in the original text, not added later.

Claims that Jesus Was a Magician or Hypnotist

It has been suggested that Jesus had learned magic tricks in Egypt and that this explained His apparent miracles. If this were true, it would mean that Jesus was attempting to deceive and manipulate the Jewish people into thinking He must be the Messiah.

This explanation is not only contrary to Jesus' character and motivation, but also fails to account for the information available to us. How would a magician bring dead people back to life, heal the man born blind, heal the paralyzed man, or restore a withered hand? This is a very feeble attempt to explain away the evidence and account for Jesus miraculous powers. It is another explanation that fails to explain.

Another excuse for avoiding the evidence of Jesus actually performing miracles is the bizarre claim that he was a hypnotist. This fails for many of the same reasons as the claim that he was a magician. It also would involve Jesus in deception contrary to his character. Neither hypnosis can explain the actual healings that took place.

Also, not everyone is susceptible to being hypnotized and many of those in the crowds would not have been susceptible. Skeptics, doubters, and opponents of Jesus would not have been subject to hypnosis. Jesus' half-brothers and Thomas were not hypnotized. Neither were the religious leaders who did not deny the miracles, but were angry that his healings violated their rules. There is the additional reality that when Jesus was no longer with them, his followers still believed in his miracles including his return from the dead.[251]

Claims that the Miracles Were Illusions

It is quite a stretch to imagine one could cause people to think he had made the wind and waves to stop or to delude a dozen men into thinking you had stopped a storm. Many of those men were fishermen who knew the weather and circumstances that could occur on that body of water. For them to be terrified was not the result of a trick or illusion. Besides that, Jesus had been asleep when the storm hit so he was not involved in their terror.

For the paralyzed man to get up and walk, for a dead man to sit up and speak, for a man's withered hand to be restored cannot be explained as illusions. These physical transformations cannot be dismissed as mere illusions. The only illusion is the skeptics willingness to believe such weak excuses as if they explain the miracles.

Claims the Gospels Contradict Each Other

There are also claims made that the Gospels contradict each other. It is assumed that if one account does not mention something, or give the exact same details as are in another account, that this is a contradiction. That is a false assumption. There is no requirement that each account parallel one another. There would only need to be one account in that case.

In fact, if they each completely agreed in what they presented including the details, the Gospel authors would be accused of collusion; that they got together to agree on what to include, how to present Jesus etc. The accounts agree in their essential information, but differ on details much like different honest witnesses to an accident or other historical event. This attack ignores the different personalities, experiences, and vocabularies of the writers, as well as the differences in their purpose and intended audience.

For there to be a genuine contradiction would require that two or more statements would be mutually exclusive, that is if one were true the other statement could not be true. This is not the case in the biblical Gospels; they vary in the details included or omitted but do not render one in actual conflict with another. In other words, the differing accounts in the Gospels are supplementary and complementary rather than contradictory.

Note that every one of these attempts to dismiss the value of the Biblical Gospels involves many assumptions, some of which are not obvious until pointed out. They each begin with the assumption that the Gospels cannot be reliable despite the lack of any genuine basis for such an assumption. Most of the attacks assume the Gospel accounts to have been altered as to essential elements despite the lack of any evidence of such tampering.

Sarcastic Humor Substituting for Evidence

Another tried and true method of deceiving people in regard to the Gospels and other biblical writings is to take something from a biblical narrative and then make sarcastic and humorous remarks about the event or statement as if that refutes the validity of the information. The famous British philosopher Bertrand Russell used this method of humorous ridicule to substitute for evidence and valid argument. So have other skeptics.

"But surely we know Jesus was born in Bethlehem? Oh dear. The place of Jesus birth also raises some problems. If we only had Mark and John to go on, we would assume it was Nazareth because they call Nazareth his hometown as Jesus does. But Luke and Matthew both set the story of Jesus birth in Bethlehem."[252]

Only Matthew and Luke specify where Jesus was born. Jesus spent probably less than a year there because of danger from Herod. Upon returning from Egypt, Joseph discovered that Herod's son, Archelaus was now ruling Judea. Therefor he did not want to risk rearing Jesus in Bethlehem. He took Mary and Jesus to Nazareth in Galilee where Jesus lived from about age three or four until he began his public ministry. That is why he was known as Jesus of Nazareth and why Nazareth was considered his hometown.

The same skeptic, then denies the references to the census and requirement of returning to one's ancestral home for taxation.[253] Then he suggests the only reason Matthew and Luke give Bethlehem as the birthplace was to make it look like Jesus fulfilled the prediction of Micah that the Messiah would be born of the house of David in Bethlehem.[254] That also discredits the character of Matthew and Luke. It would never occur to this type of critic, that Matthew and Luke might just be giving greater detail than the other writers.

False Statements in Regard to the New Testament

Another approach, also used by Russell as well as others is to make up statements saying the Bible says this or doesn't say that. In most of those cases, actually reading the Bible reveals the deception of the critic. Of course, they assume most people will not read the New Testament writings of the Bible (unfortunately true), and so they will generally get away with the deception. Most people will just assume the skeptic is correct and will repeat the criticism to others rather than checking for themselves.

Another example is to change the wording of scripture. Crossan claims his translations of Jesus words are based upon his understanding of Jesus as a Mediterranean Jewish peasant. An example is Jesus words in Luke 9:58: "*Foxes have holes and birds of the air have nests; but the Son of man has nowhere to lay his head.*" He gives the following as his translation: "*Every fox has a den. Every bird has a nest. Only humans are homeless.*"[255]

Claims that Jesus' Genealogies Are Contradictory

Matthew 1:1-16 and Luke 3:23-38 present different genealogies of Jesus. Some skeptics have claimed the two genealogies contradict one another. However, they are not contradictory. The genealogy in Matthew is that of Joseph, the supposed or stepfather of Jesus. Joseph is a descendent of David through the kingly linage of his son Solomon. The purpose of this genealogy is to show Jesus legal right to the throne of Israel.

The genealogy in Luke is that through His mother, Mary who is also a descendent of David through David's son Nathan. This indicates that Jesus is also an actual descendent of David. Both Mary and Joseph were descendants of David through different sons. The significance of the genealogies is due to God's promises that a descendant of David would be king forever (2Samuel 7:12-16; Isaiah 9:6-7; 16:5). They indicate that Jesus, the future king will be the fulfillment of these promises to David and Israel.

Claims that Biblical Interpretation Can Justify Anything

It has been stated by critics that you can interpret the Bible to mean whatever you want. The conclusion is then made that there is therefore no reason to take it seriously. This is again a very deceptive argument. It is true that by ignoring reason, logic, and basic rules of literary interpretation you can make the Bible say whatever you want. But using the same methods such critics apply to the Bible to other literature would make nonsense of the other writings as well – including their own writings. But they only apply their absence of basic principles of reason and interpretation to the Bible.

For example, they ignore historical context which enables them to take a statement or teaching in one era and contradict it with a statement or principle from a totally different historical situation and time, claiming it proves a contradiction. Another favorite tactic is to take a biblical statement out of its immediate literary context in order to misinterpret or misapply it in contrast to another biblical statement (also often out of context) order to create the appearance of a contradiction.

There is also the method of making general criticisms or attacks against the Bible without giving any specific reference. The statement is made that the Bible teaches this or the Bible is against that without any specific reference as justification for the statement. It is assumed that since the vast majority of people will never read the biblical writings that these false statements about it or attributed to it will be believed.

Another tactic of some critics is to pretend there is information that does not exist. For example, it has been claimed that Jesus wrote a book in which he declared that he was not the Messiah. Such a book cannot be found because it does not exist. Another of these false claims is that what is probably the remains of Jesus have been found.

Another false claim is that the Church has hidden information that contradicts the validity of its biblical teachings. For example, it is asserted that the church hid or destroyed information that disproved the resurrection of Jesus from the dead. Once again it may need to be stated that anything can be declared or claimed but what does the evidence reveal? There is no evidence that such a repression or destruction of evidence has occurred.

In fact, the reality is that without the genuineness of the resurrection there would not ever have been a church. It is important to realize that the Church did not create the scriptures (though the Roman Catholic Church makes this claim). The Apostles preaching and teaching which is recorded for us in the biblical scriptures created the Church. Without the Resurrection and the apostles teaching of it, there would not have been a church and there would have been no New Testament Scriptures.

As to the Resurrection teaching, remember that the resurrection of Jesus was first proclaimed right in Jerusalem at Pentecost, just forty days after Jesus had been executed there. This was not some mere claim begun in a distant corner of the empire, or made decades later. The resurrection was proclaimed right where everyone knew what had happened only a few weeks earlier. A critic may retort that this is what the Bible states, but the Bible cannot be trusted.

How do we know the critic can be trusted? He or she wants to discount the only evidence we actually do have because of their own bias in support of statements completely lacking in evidence. The empty tomb, the appearances of Jesus, and the transformed lives of Jesus disciples that followed his appearances cannot be dismissed on the basis of scholarship without an evaluation of the evidence. The biblical Gospels are historical documents and deserve to be evaluated as one would any other ancient historical documents.

There are complete books that carefully analyze the evidence for the resurrection and show that the resurrection to be better authenticated than most of ancient history that is readily accepted as genuine.[256] Some of those evidences of the resurrection will be summarized in 'Appendix D at the end of this publication. That will be a survey rather than a complete recounting of the evidence in detail which would require an entire book. There are many such books giving the evidence in detail.

Often, critics need to be more critical of their own thinking and even of their reading. Some critics assert something that is clearly not in the text they refer to. Other skeptics miss or ignore what is definitely present in the text.

An example of this is the critic's statements that Jesus never claimed to be the Messiah. However, John 4:25-26 reads as follows, *"The women said to him, 'I know that Messiah is coming (He who is called the Christ); when He comes, He will declare all things to us.' Jesus said to her, I who speak to you am He.'"* In Matthew 24:5, speaking to his disciples, Jesus said *"For many will come in my name saying 'I am the Christ'*, and will mislead many."* Christ is from the Greek word meaning Messiah. There are also other direct as well as indirect claims of Jesus to be the Messiah in Mark 13:6; Luke 21:8; 22:67; John 8:24, 28; 13:19.

The problem is with the critics, not in the New Testament biblical writings. The actual issue is that the Biblical worldview clashes with and contradicts the naturalistic worldview assumptions of the critics. Were the critics willing and able to lay aside their worldview assumptions, their biases, and preferences, and consider the Gospels and other New Testament documents on their own merits they would come to very different conclusions than they currently make.

Jesus Would not Refer to Himself in the Third Person

Another criticism is that since Jesus is teaching in the presence of His disciples and the crowds, He would not refer to Himself in the third person. Based upon that assumption, it is then asserted that when Jesus uses the words "Son of Man" He must be speaking of someone other than Himself. However, reading these actual statements of Jesus, it is obvious that He is speaking of Himself.

This argument is also used to claim that the use of the third person may indicate this was a later writer putting words into Jesus' mouth. It is, however, evident that writers, when speaking frequently of themselves do sometimes use the third person rather than always saying I or me.

For example: Matthew 8:19-20. *Then a scribe came and said to Him, "Teacher, I will follow You wherever You go." Jesus said to him, "The foxes have holes and the birds of the air have nests, but the Son of Man has nowhere to lay his head."* Jesus is giving the scribe an example of the hardship he will face to truly follow Him. He is obviously referring to himself.

Matthew 9:5-6 *"Which is easier to say, 'Your sins are forgiven,' or to say, 'Get up and walk'? But so that you may know that the Son of Man has authority on earth to forgive sins" – then He said to the paralytic, "Get up, pick up your bed and go home."* Here Jesus certainly claims to be the Son of man who can forgive sins.

Matt 20:18 *"Behold we are going up to Jerusalem; and the Son of Man will be delivered to the chief priests and scribes and they will condemn Him to death."* Jesus is obviously speaking of Himself. See also a related example at Luke 18:31-33.

That We Are All Sons of God

Our perusal of the Gospels refutes another favorite but false idea of some so-called Liberal theologians and leaders of other religions such as the New Age. That false idea is the erroneous claim that we are all sons of God in the same way as Jesus. It is difficult to imagine how anyone who pays attention while reading these Gospels can pretend that they or anyone else can compare themselves with the person of Jesus.

That Jesus is the unique Son of God is a clear teaching of the Biblical scriptures—there is no other human being like Him. He who is God from all eternity, took on also a human nature and body to live a perfect human life in order to die for the sins of all the rest of us. There never was and will never be another like Him.

God is the Father of all in the sense of being the creator and giver of life. But God is not the Father of all in terms of relationship and family. It is another clear teaching of the Bible that only those who come to Christ by faith are included as sons (and daughters) of God, but still not in the same sense as Jesus is. By our faith in Jesus, we are adopted into the family of God. (John 1:12-13; 3:16; Galatians 3:22, 24, 26; Ephesians 1:5; 2:12, 19; 1John 4:15; 5:11-12).

The Claim that the Synoptic Gospels Present a Merely Human Jesus

Another frequent claim of skeptics and liberal theologians is that while the writings of the apostle Paul, and the assumed to be later, Gospel of John present Jesus a divine, implying that this is a later addition or alteration, the Synoptic Gospels show him as merely a human teacher and prophet. There have even been groups who have apparently studied the Synoptic Gospels who have declared this misperception to be the case.[257]

The Synoptic Gospels are the first three in the New Testament; Matthew, Mark, and Luke. We will examine all three of these books including the repetitions to show that they each teach a divine Jesus. Each of these gospels has a unique purpose as well as supporting the full humanity and full Deity of Jesus. You are not being asked to accept the Deity of Christ, though that would be wonderful, but you are being asked to see that, that is the obvious teaching of each of the Biblical Gospels.

Matthew was written primarily to the Jews as a transition between the Old and New Testaments. Mark is considered to have been written particularly to the Romans and as the earliest Gospel, thus closest to the original events. Luke was written especially to the Greeks and was based upon historical research by him to verify the precise truth.

It is important at this point to remind readers that this segment of the publication is not to prove the Bible is God's word, though the author is confident that it is. The purpose here is to carefully attend to that which the Gospels actually teach. It is essential at this point to take what the passages say, rather than reading into them what one wants or expects them to present.

Other sections of this publication deal with the issue of Divine authorship and authority of these writings. The process here will be to go through specific texts of each of the Synoptic Gospels to refute the claim that they do not present a divine Jesus. We will go through each of these three Gospels separately and sequentially. Also note that some of the references clearly indicate Jesus to be God, whereas there are also references that hint or suggest his deity.

As you will discover if you read through any one of the Gospels, much like the skeptics of today, the religious leaders oppose the challenge Jesus is to their authority and hypocrisy. They ignore the reality of the good he miraculously accomplishes and the evidence it sheds upon His true identity.

Many of the quotes from the Gospels are long, and some I have repeated from the separate Gospels. Never-the-less, I have felt it essential to quote these passages in detail rather than merely giving the references. This is because I anticipate that many people would not bother to actually look up the passages. Many would either just accept or reject what I say about them without being impacted by what each Gospel reveals about Jesus' identity without reading the passage.

The Gospel of Matthew

1:20-23. *"Now the birth of Jesus Christ was as follows: when his mother Mary had been betrothed to Joseph, before they came together, she was found to be with child by the Holy Spirit. ... an angel of the Lord appeared to him in a dream saying 'Joseph, son of David do not be afraid to take Mary as your wife; for the child who has been conceived in her is of the Holy Spirit. She will bear a Son; and you shall call his name Jesus, for He will save His people from their sins' Now all this took place to fulfill what was spoken by the Lord* *through the prophet: 'Behold, the virgin shall be with child and shall bear a son, and they shall call his name Immanuel,' which translated means 'God with us.'"*

The Holy Spirit is clearly shown in both the Old and New Testaments to be God so it is obvious this was to be a divinely initiated conception and birth. A virgin conceiving, apart from human sexual contact is again a claim of God's intervention. Another claim is that this is in fulfillment of Divine prophecy and his names indicate this Jesus is both Savior and God.

2:11. "*After coming into the house they saw the child with Mary His mother, and worshipped Him.*" Worship was normally reserved for one thought to be God.

3:2-3. "*Repent, for the kingdom of heaven is at hand." For this is the one referred to by Isaiah the prophet when he said, "The voice of one crying in the wilderness, 'Make ready the way of the Lord, make His paths straight.'"* These are the words of John the Baptist who quotes from Isaiah 40:3 referring to preparing the way in advance for God to visit His people. Matthew is presenting John as fulfilling this prophecy as the messenger preparing the way for Jesus, thus indicating that God has come in the person of Jesus.

3:16-17. "*After being baptized, Jesus came up from the water; and behold, the heavens were opened, and he swathe Spirit of God descending as a dove and lighting on Him, and behold, a voice out of the heavens said, 'This is my beloved Son, in whom I am well pleased.'"*

Neither the Spirit lighting on him nor the voice out of heaven happened at other baptisms. The events as well as the designation of "My Son" indicates the unique relationship of Jesus with God the Father.

5:17. "*Do not think that I came to abolish the Law or the Prophets; I did not come to abolish but to fulfill.*"

This saying of Jesus is a declaration that He is the fulfillment of the Law and Prophets. See the list of prophecies in Appendix A. For Jesus to be the fulfillment of these scriptures indicates he is more than merely a human teacher and prophet.

7:21-23. *Not everyone who says to Me, "Lord, Lord" will enter the kingdom of heaven, but he who does the will of My Father who is in heaven will enter. Many will say to me on that day, "Lord, Lord, did we not prophecy in your name, and in your name cast out demons and, in Your name, perform many miracles?" And then I will declare to them, "I never knew you; depart from Me, you who practice lawlessness."*

Jesus calls Himself Lord which is a hint that he is more than a mere man. If these false prophets thought Jesus was merely a human teacher or prophet, they would not be prophesying and claiming to do miracles in his name. If He were not God, those persons would not be appealing to Him at the judgment. To be using His name as the authority and source for their actions, was acknowledging Him to be God.[258]

7:28-29 *"When Jesus had finished these words, the crowds were amazed at his teaching; for He was teaching them as one having authority, and not like their scribes."* Jesus did not refer to one of the prophets as his authority, nor to one of the other rabbis recognized as authoritative by the Jews, but spoke as being the authority Himself.

8:8, 13. *"But the centurion said, 'Lord I am not worthy for You to come under my roof, but just say the word, and my servant will be healed. ...' And Jesus said to the centurion, 'Go; it shall be done for you as you have believed.' And the servant was healed that very moment."*

So, the words of Jesus are sufficient to bring instant healing for the servant even from a distance. Jesus is not in physical proximity to the man, but speaks the reality into existence from where he and the centurion are. No mere human could affect a healing from a distance. He had to be God to know where the servant was and which servant needed healing.

8:26-27. *"He said to them, 'Why are you afraid, you men of little faith?' Then He got up and rebuked the winds and the sea and it became perfectly calm. The men were amazed and said, 'What kind of man is this, that even the winds and the sea obey Him?'"* Power over the strong forces of nature strongly suggests Jesus to be the Lord over all the earth, its Creator. Unlike the prophets who prayed, calling on God to do something, Jesus acted here as the authority over nature Himself.

Matthew 8:29-32. *"And they cried out, saying, 'What business do we have with each other, Son of God? Have you come here to torment us before the time?' ... The demons began to* entreat Him, saying, 'If you are going to cast us out, send us into the herd of swine.' And He said to them, 'Go!' And they came out and went into the swine, and the whole herd rushed down the steep bank into the sea and perished in the waters." The demons were obviously afraid of Jesus, acknowledge Him as the Son of God and that they had no choice but to obey Him.

9:2-6. "And they brought to Him a paralytic lying on a bed. Seeing their faith, Jesus said to the paralytic, 'Take courage, son; your sins are forgiven.' And some of the scribes said to themselves, 'This fellow blasphemes.' And Jesus knowing their thoughts said, 'Why are you thinking evil in your hearts? Which is easier to say, 'Your sins are forgiven' or to say, 'Get up and walk? But so that you may know that the Son of Man has authority on earth to forgive sins—then He said to the paralytic 'Get up, pick up your bed and go home.' And he got up and went home. But when the crowds saw this, they were awestruck and glorified God who had given such authority to men."

It was obviously easier to say "Your sins are forgiven," because there was no objective way to prove or disprove whether it was so. However, this was not something a first century Jewish person would even think apart from providing the required animal sacrifice at the temple, unless He was the One who truly could forgive sin. Jesus recognizes the skepticism of the scribes and so he heals the man to verify that the former paralytic's sins were actually forgiven.

Jesus heals by merely saying the words, much like the original creation by God in Genesis 1. The Pharisees were correct that only God can forgive sin. They didn't realize the truth that Jesus was God as well as man. The title Jesus uses here and frequently for Himself, "Son of Man" is messianic, used in Daniel 7 and also by the prophet Ezekiel.

As you discover when you read through the gospels, much like the skeptics of today, the religious leaders question and reject Jesus' authority because He challenges their authority and reputations. He revealed their hypocrisy. They ignore the reality of the good he miraculously accomplishes, as well as the evidence it sheds upon who He really is.

Matt. 9:18, 19, 23-25. "While He was saying these things to them, a synagogue official came and bowed down before Him and said, 'My daughter has just died; but come and lay Your *hand on her and she will live.' Jesus got up and began to follow him and so did His disciples. ... When Jesus came into the official's house and saw the flute players and the crowd in noisy disorder, He said, 'Leave for the girl has no died but is asleep.' And they began laughing at Him. But when the crowd had been sent out, He entered and took her by the hand and the girl got up."*

Who has the power over life and death? This is an example of the power of God. Jesus does not need to pray or plead with God, not perform any religious rituals. He merely takes her hand and immediately His almighty power recalls her spirit to her body.

Matt. 10:1. *"Jesus summoned His twelve disciples and gave them authority over unclean spirits, to cast them out, and to heal every kind of disease and every kind of sickness."* If Jesus were a mere man, how would he be able to bestow such power and authority upon others that they could perform miracles? Jesus temporarily bestowed some of his power and authority upon them. This is another sign of his Deity.

Matt. 11:9-10. *"But what did you go out to see? A prophet? Yes, I tell you, and one who is more than a prophet. This is the one about whom it is written, 'Behold, I send my messenger ahead of You, who will prepare Your way before You.'"* Jesus was speaking of John the Baptist as the messenger that preceded him in the fulfillment of the prophecy in Malachi 3:1 and following. If you read that prophecy, it is of God speaking regarding His coming to the people and His temple to be preceded by a messenger.

Matt. 11:27. *"All things have been handed over to me by my Father; and no one knows the Son except the Father; nor does anyone know the Father except the Son, and anyone to whom the Son wills to reveal Him."* Jesus is claiming such an intimate relationship with the Father, that the Father has entrusted all thing unto Him. Jesus is also saying that to genuinely know God does not come about through human wisdom, intuition, religious practices, nor by any other means including even reading scripture, unless the Son reveals the Father to us by His own will. He has claimed to have the sole authority to reveal God to humanity.

Matt. 11:28-29. *"Come to Me, all who are weary and heavy-laden, and I will give you rest. Take My yoke upon you and learn from Me, for I am gentle and humble in heart, and you shall find rest for your souls*." The last phrase "you shall find rest for your souls," is a quote from Jeremiah 6:16 where the speaker is God. Who is Jesus claiming to be with this statement?

Matt. 12:6, 8. "*But I say to you that something greater than the temple is here. ... For the Son of Man is Lord of the Sabbath.*" Here Jesus first makes the claim to be greater than the temple at which God was worshipped, and then asserts that He is the Lord of the Sabbath which was instituted by God in Exodus 20:8-11 as one of the Ten Commandments. Jesus has here made an unambiguous claim to be God!

Matt. 12:39-41. *But he answered and said to them, "An evil and adulterous generation craves for a sign; and no sign will be given to it but the sign of Jonah the prophet; for just as Jonah was three days and three nights in the belly of the sea monster, so will the Son of Man be three days and three nights in the heart of the earth. The men of Nineveh will stand up with this generation at the judgment and will condemn it because they repented at the preaching of Jonah; and behold, something greater than Jonah is here.*"

Jesus claims to be greater than Jonah, certainly one of the most successful prophets of Israel and predicts his own death and resurrection as symbolized by the events that happened to Jonah. Who is Jesus claiming to be by these statements?

Matt. 12:42. Jesus is continuing to teach, "*The Queen of the South will rise up with this generation at the judgment and will condemn it, because she came from the ends of the earth to hear the wisdom of Solomon; and behold something greater than Solomon is here.*"

In this passage, Jesus is referring to the events recorded in 1Kings 10. In reference to that Old Testament reference, Jesus claims to be greater than the wise king Solomon.

Matt. 13:41. "*The Son of Man will send forth His angels, and they will gather out of His kingdom all stumbling blocks and those who commit lawlessness ...*" What kingdom does Jesus proclaim and explain? Whose kingdom is it? To whom do the angels belong and obey? What does He imply by calling the angels 'His'?

Matt. 15:33 "*And those who were in the boat worshipped Him, saying 'You certainly are God's Son!'*" Jesus had much earlier declared that only God was to be worshipped (Matt. 4:10). None of the prophets accepted worship, neither did Jesus disciples then nor after his ascension. See Acts 10:25-26; 14:11-18. No merely human orthodox Jew would have accepted worship. Notice that Jesus does not respond by disclaiming their statement as to His identity, nor did He reject their worship. Jesus accepted worship when it was given. See other times when Jesus accepted worship: Matt. 8:2; 14:33; 28:9,17; John 9:18.

Matt. 16:15-17. "*He said to them, 'But who do you say that I am?' Simon Peter answered, 'You are the Christ, the Son of the living God.'. And Jesus said to him, 'Blessed are you, Simon Bar-Jonah because flesh and blood did not reveal this to you, but My Father who is in heaven.'*" In answer to the question, Peter asserts that Jesus is the Messiah and the Son of God. Jesus commends Peter for that awareness he has received from God, the Father. Jesus accepts both designations that Peter has expressed.

Matt. 16:27. "*For the Son of Man, is going to come in the glory of His Father with His angels, and will then repay every man according to his deeds.*"

Matt. 18:20. "*For where two or three have gathered together in My name, I am there in their midst.*" Jesus tells his disciples that he is present with them in some special way when they gather in His name. Jesus doesn't say this in regard to those who gather in the name of God or of the Father, but in His name. What does that tell us about his own self-awareness?

Matt. 21:16 "*Do you hear what these children are saying? Jesus said to them, 'Yes; have you never read, 'Out of the mouth of infants and nursing babies you have prepared praise for yourself?'*" In answer to the religious leader's complaint about the children shouting praise to Jesus in the temple, Jesus quotes Psalm 8:2. If you read Psalm 8:1-2 you discover that Jesus is quoting a statement attributed to God and applying it to Himself. So once again, Jesus is clearly declaring Himself to be God.

Matt. 23:34 "*Therefore, behold, I am sending you prophets and wise men and scribes; some of them you will kill and crucify, and some of them you will scourge in your synagogues, and persecute from city to city …*" Jesus declares that He is the one who will be sending these prophets and others who will be thus persecuted by the Jewish religious leaders. If it is He who will send these prophets who is He claiming to be?

Matt. 24:30-31. *"And then the sign of the Son of Man will appear in the sky, and then all the tribes of the earth will mourn, and they will see the Son of Man coming on the clouds of the sky with power and great glory. And He will send forth His angels with a great trumpet and they will gather together His elect from the four winds, from one end of the sky to the other."*

Teaching in regard to the end times, Jesus declares that the populace of the earth will mourn when they realize He really is returning. Why would they respond in that way? Then He does not merely claim He will return, but that He will return with a great display of power and glory. Next, He states that His angels will be sent at His instruction to gather His elect from throughout the earth. If the angels are His and they follow His orders, who is He claiming to be? If those who are gathered from throughout the earth belong to Him, who is He? None of the human prophets of Israel made such claims for themselves, as Jesus makes.

Matt. 24:35. "Heaven and earth will pass away, but My words will not pass away." Speaking around 30 A.D., how could Jesus' claim to know the present physical universe would end? If this creation ceases to exist, but His words still remain, must He not be claiming to be the Creator?

Matt. 24:37, 42. *"For the coming of the Son of Man will be just like the days of Noah ... Therefore, be on the alert, for you do not know which day your Lord is coming."* Jesus is continuing to speak of the end times, and He uses the frequent title for Himself as the Son of Man. He tells what will be occurring on the earth at the time of His return to it. He then warns His followers to be anticipating Him, as their Lord. See also, 24:44, 25:13.

Matt. 25:31-34. *"But when the Son of Man comes in His glory, and all the angels with Him, then He will sit on His glorious throne. And all the nations will be gathered before Him; and He will separate them from one another, as the shepherd separates the sheep from the goats; and He will put the sheep on His right and the goats on His left. Then the king will say to those on His right 'Come, you who are blessed of my*

Father, inherit the kingdom prepared for you from the foundation of the world.'"

Jesus stated that He will come in glory with all the angels, will sit on His kingly throne and judge the nations. That is obviously a role of God. See Psa. 2:6-12.

Matt. 26:64 Jesus said to him, '*You have said it yourself; nevertheless I tell you, hereafter you shall see the Son of Man sitting at the right hand of power, and coming on the clouds of heaven.*" Psa. 110:1; Dan. 7:13.

Matt. 28:9 "*And behold, Jesus met them and greeted them. And they came up and took hold of His feet and worshipped Him.*" This is following Jesus' execution, burial, and resurrection. Jesus appears to these women who had been His followers and accepts their worship. Remember these are strict monotheists! See also 28:17.

Matt. 28:18-20. "*And Jesus came up and spoke to them, saying, 'All authority has been given to Me in heaven and on earth. Go therefore and make disciples of all the nations, baptizing them in the name of the Father and the Son and the Holy Spirit, teaching them to observe all that I commanded you; and lo, I am with you always, even to the end of the age.'"*

These verses are loaded with evidence that Jesus is presented as God. This is also a very clear indication that God exists as three distinct personalities though one God, and that Jesus is one of those personalities. He has been given ultimate authority in heaven as well as earth. The disciple making of His followers is in the name of the Father, Son, and Holy Spirit. Linking the Son and Holy Spirit with the Father indicates they are equals. The promise that His presence is always with them to the end of the age would require Him to be the eternal God.

The Gospel of Mark

Mark 1:1-3. "*The beginning of the gospel of Jesus Christ, the Son of God. As it is written in Isaiah the prophet: 'Behold I send my messenger ahead of you, who will prepare your way; The voice of one crying in the wilderness, Make ready the way of the Lord, make His paths straight'"*

This reference to Isaiah 40:3 is in regard to a messenger preparing the way in advance for God to come to His people. John was preparing the way for Jesus to visibly reveal and demonstrate the character and compassion of the invisible God.

Mark 1:10-11. *"Immediately coming up out of the water, He saw the heavens opening and the Spirit like a dove descending upon Him; and a voice came out of the heavens: 'You are my beloved Son, in You I am well-pleased.'"*

Mark 1:23-26. *"Just then there was a man in their synagogue with an unclean spirit and he cried out, saying, 'What business do we have with each other, Jesus of Nazareth? Have You come to destroy us? I know who You are—the Holy One of God!' And Jesus rebuked him, saying, 'Be quiet, and come out of him!' Throwing him into convulsions, the unclean spirit cried out with a loud voice and came out of him."*

The evil spirit acknowledges who Jesus is and that Jesus has authority, even to destroy it. The spirit obeys Jesus' command.

Mark 2:5-12. *"And Jesus seeing their faith said to the paralytic, 'Son your sins are forgiven.' ... 'Why does this man speak that way? He is blaspheming; who can forgive sins but God alone?' ... 'But so that you may know that the Son of Man has authority on earth to forgive sins' – He said to the paralytic, 'I say to you, get up, pick up your pallet and go home.' And he got up and immediately picked up the pallet and went out in the sight of everyone, so that they were amazed and were glorifying God, saying, 'We have never seen anything like this.'"*

Mark 2:28 *"Jesus said to them, 'The Sabbath was made for man, and not man for the Sabbath. So the Son of Man is Lord even of the Sabbath.'"* Shortly after the establishment of the Sabbath, Moses mentions a reason for it in Exodus 23:12. This illustrates that the Sabbath was made for man. Since the Sabbath was established by God, to claim to be Lord of the Sabbath is a claim to be God.

Mark 3:3-5. *"He said to the man with the withered hand, 'Get up and come forward!' And He said to them, 'Is it lawful to do good or to do harm on the Sabbath, to save a life or to kill?' But they kept silent. After looking around at them with anger, grieved at their hardness of heart, He said to the man, 'Stretch out your hand.' And he stretched it out, and his hand was restored.*"

This was obviously not a psychosomatic healing, nor an illusion or magic trick. Jesus enacted a miraculous healing by merely telling the man to stretch out his hand. This reveals not only the power of God but also His compassion. Much like skeptics of today, the Pharisees were only concerned about their authority and reputations rather than the truth and the benefit to the individual.

Mark 3:11-12. "*Whenever the unclean spirits saw Him they would fall down before Him and shout, "You are the Son of God." And He earnestly warned them not to tell who He was.*"

Again, we are shown that the demons knew who Jesus is and that they are subject to His authority. Falling down before Him is not likely something they would have chosen to do if they had, had the choice.

Mark 4:37-41. "*And there arose a fierce gale of wind, and the waves were breaking over the boat so much that the boat was already filling up. Jesus Himself was in the stern, asleep on the cushion; and they woke Him and said to Him, 'Teacher, do You not care that we are perishing?' And He got up and rebuked the wind and said to the sea, 'Hush, be still.' And the wind died down and it became perfectly calm. And He said to them, 'Why are you afraid? Do you still have no faith?' They became very much afraid and said to one another, 'Who then is this, that even the wind and sea obey Him?'*"

Indeed, who is this that even the wind and the sea obey Him? Even the seasoned fishermen among them were terrified at the ferocity of the storm and the prospect of sinking. The Creator did not fear the forces of nature that He had created. Creation was and is still subject to His authority and control if He chooses to intervene.

Mark 5:2-3, 6-8, 11-13, 15, 19-20. "*When He got out of the boat, immediately a man from the tombs with an unclean spirit met Him. And he had his dwelling among the tombs, and no one was able to bind him anymore, even with a chain ... Seeing Jesus from a distance, he ran up and bowed down before Him; and shouting with a loud voice, he said, 'What business do we have with each other, Jesus, Son of the most High God? I implore You, by God, do not torment me!' For He had* been saying to him, 'Come out of the man, you unclean spirit! ... 'Now there was a large herd of swine feeding nearby on the mountain. The demons implored Him, saying, 'Send us into the swine so that we may enter them.' Jesus gave them permission. ... The people came to see what it was that had happened. They came to Jesus and observed the man who had been demon possessed sitting down, clothed and in his right mind, the very man who had the 'legion' and they became frightened."*

"As He was getting into the boat, the man who had been demon-possessed was imploring Him that he might accompany Him. And He did not let him, but He said to him, 'Go home to your people and report to them what great things the Lord has done for you and how He had mercy on you.' And he went away and began to proclaim in Decapolis what great things Jesus had done for him; and everyone was amazed."

The demons were submitted, afraid of Jesus and acknowledged who He is. The man was delivered from them all and his humanity restored. Jesus is presented as being the Lord, which is most often shown in scripture to be a reference to God.

Mark 5:35-36, 39-43. *"While He was still speaking, they came from the house of the synagogue official saying, 'Your daughter has died; why trouble the teacher anymore?' But Jesus, overhearing what was being spoken, said to the synagogue official, 'Do not be afraid any longer, only believe.' ... and entering in, He said to them, 'Why make a commotion and weep? The child has not died, but is asleep.' They began laughing at Him. But putting them all out, He took along the child's father and mother and His own companions, and entered the room where the child was. Taking the child by the hand, He said to her, 'Talitha koum!' (which translated means, "Little girl, I say to you, get up). Immediately the girl got up and began to walk, for she was twelve years old. And immediately they were completely astounded. And He gave them strict orders that no one should know about this, and he said that something should be given her to eat."*

This is most likely the same event that was recorded in Matthew 9:22-26. Jesus is presented as having authority and power over death itself and the restoration of life is immediate. Resuscitations were extremely rare in the

Scriptures and certainly required the power of God. This example seen in the light of the vast amount of other evidence, implies that Jesus is God.

Mark 6:37-44. *"But He answered them, 'You give them something to eat.' And they said to Him, 'Shall we go and spend two hundred denarii on bread and give them something to eat?' And He said to them, 'How many loaves do you have, Go look!' And when they found out, they said, 'Five and two fish.' And He commanded them all to sit down by groups on the green grass. ... And He took the five loaves and the two fish, and looking toward heaven, He blessed the food and broke the loaves and He kept giving them to the disciples to set before them; and he divided up the two fish among them all. And they all ate and were satisfied, and they picked up twelve full baskets of the broken pieces and also of the fish. There were five thousand men who ate the loaves."*

This is another account of Jesus miraculously feeding the multitude that followed him (See: Matthew 14:15-21; Luke 9:12-17). The people were without food and the disciples had very little. Jesus acted with compassion and multiplied the available food to be more than enough meet their needs. He acted here as the Creator.

Mark 6:48-51. *"Seeing them straining at the oars, for the wind was against them, at about the fourth watch of the night He came to them, walking on the sea; and He intended to pass by them. But when they saw Him walking on the sea, they supposed it was a ghost, and cried out; for they all saw Him and were terrified. But immediately He spoke with them and said to them, 'Take courage; it is I, do not be afraid.' Then He got into the boat with them, and the wind stopped; and they were utterly astonished."*

Supernatural features of this passage: Though it was late at night, and the disciples were partway across the sea of Galilee, Jesus could see the difficulty, they were having. Then he walks on the water to where they are and when He enters the boat the contrary wind ceased. This Jesus was obviously not portrayed by Mark as a mere prophet and rabbi.

Mark 7:26-30. *"Now the woman was a Gentile, of the Syrophoenician race. And she kept asking Him to cast the demon out of her daughter. And He kept saying to her, 'Let the children be satisfied first, for it is not good to take the* children's bread and throw it to the dogs.' But she answered and said to Him, 'Yes, Lord, but even the dogs under the table feed on the children's crumbs.' And He said to her, 'Because of this answer go; the demon has gone out of your daughter.' And going back to her home, she found the child lying on the bed, the demon having left."

Jesus' authority and power was such that He could cause things to occur without being in the actual location where the results took place. He had to know who the daughter was, as well as her location in order to expel the demon. Jesus is again portrayed as the omnipotent God.

Mark 8:2-9. "'I feel compassion for the people because they have remained with me now three days and have nothing to eat. If I send them away hungry to their homes, they will faint on the way; and some of them have come from a great distance.' And His disciples answered Him, 'Where will anyone be able to find enough bread here in the desolate place to satisfy these people?' And He was asking them, 'How many loaves do you have?' And they said 'Seven.' And He directed the people to sit down on the ground; and taking the seven loaves, He gave thanks and broke them, and started giving them to His disciples to serve to them, and they served them to the people. ... And they ate and were satisfied; and the picked up seven large baskets full of what was left over of the broken pieces. About four thousand were there; and He sent them away."

Not a repeat of the earlier feeding, but a separate and similar event which again presented Jesus as the compassionate Creator. It also demonstrates how difficult it is for humans to grasp the evidence right in front of us of spiritual realities (see 8:15-21).

Mark 8:38. "For whoever is ashamed of Me and My words in this adulterous and sinful generation, the Son of Man will also be ashamed of him when He comes in the glory of His Father with the Holy angels." Jesus declares that He is to return in the glory of the Father and accompanied by the angels. This would seem to be an obvious statement of His deity.

Mark 9:2, 4-7, 9. "Six days later, Jesus took with Him Peter, and James and John, and brought them up on a high mountain by themselves. And He was transfigured before them, ... Elijah appeared to them along with Moses; and they were talking with Jesus. ... Then a cloud formed *overshadowing them, and a voice came out of the cloud, 'This is My beloved Son, listen to Him!' … As they were coming down from the mountain, He gave them orders not to relate to anyone what they had seen until the Son of Man rose from the dead."*

Jesus is transformed so the three see His glory and two major figures of the Old Testament era appear to talk with Jesus. Peter feeling like he needed to say something has just spoken nonsense which diminished the significance of what the three disciples had just experienced. The Father speaks out of the cloud to remind them who the authority is. Then Jesus forbids them to tell of the experience and informs them He will rise from the dead. The Father validates who Jesus is and then Jesus foretells a future event to occur in His earthly life, His return from death which will also be a fulfillment of prophecy. Each of these inform us of Jesus deity.

Mark 9:12. *"And He said to them, 'Elijah does come first and restore all things. And yet how is it written of the Son of Man that He will suffer many things and be treated with contempt?'"* In this verse Jesus has indicated that previous writings (in the Old Testament) are about the suffering He is about to endure (For example see: Psa. 22; Isa. 52:13-53:12). He knows in advance what is to happen to Him and that it fulfills the Old Testament prophecies about Him.

Mark 10:33-34. *"Behold, we are going up to Jerusalem, and the Son of Man will be delivered to the chief priests and the scribes; and they will condemn Him to death and will hand Him over to the Gentiles. They will mock Him and spite on Him, and scourge Him and kill Him, and three days later He will rise again."*

He who has raised the dead is declaring his death and resurrection from the dead after three days. He began referring to His death and resurrection immediately following Peter's declaration of Jesus to be the Christ (Messiah). See also 8:31; 9:9; 9:31; 10:33-34; 14:27-28. Notice that He knows what is going to happen and does nothing to attempt to avoid or prevent it, because it is the plan of the Father in order to provide eternal life for us (Mark 10:45)

Mark 13:5-6, 13, 21-23. *"And Jesus began to say to them, 'See to it that no one misleads you. Many will come in My name, saying 'I am He!' and will mislead many. … You will be hated by all because of my name, but the one who endures to the end, he will be saved, … And then if anyone says to you, 'Behold, here is the Christ'; or, 'Behold, He is there'; do not believe him; for false Christs and false prophets will arise, and will show signs and wonders, in order to lead astray, if possible, the elect. But take heed; behold, I have told you everything in advance."*

How does Jesus know that in the future many will come professing to be Him? Who is He claiming to be in these statements? Why would some people hate followers of Jesus? Who is He that is the Source of salvation? Note that miraculous signs are not in themselves sufficient proof of His identity. This links with the following verses that tell some of the conditions or events preceding His return in 13:24-25.

Mark 13:26-27. *"Then they will see the Son of Man coming in clouds with great power and glory. And then He will send forth the angels, and will gather together His elect from the four winds, from the farthest end of the earth to the farthest end of heaven."* He not only claims that He will return, but that His return will be obvious to the world. Not only that, He is to return in power and glory. He is to direct the actions of the angels. Though He, Himself has travelled in a very limited segment of the earth, He claims that his elect, His followers will exist all over the earth. Is it not clear that Mark is presenting Jesus as God?

Mark 13:31. *"Heaven and earth will pass away, but my words will not pass away."* He declares that the heavens and earth will cease to exist but His word will endure even that destruction. This is a continuation of Jesus' claims to know the future as well as a claim that His word will outlive the destruction of our world.

Mark 14:21. *"For the Son of Man is to go just as it is written of Him; but woe to that man by whom the Son of Man is betrayed it would have been good for that man if he had not been born."* "As it is written of Him" is in reference to the prophecies of the Old Testament which Jesus says are about Him. Also, He knows He is being betrayed and who the betrayer is but does nothing to prevent the betrayal because it is in the purpose of both Jesus and the Father. (See verses: 18-20, 27, 36; Matt. 26:25).

Mark 14:61-64. *"But He kept silent, and did not answer. Again the high priest was questioning Him, and saying to Him, 'Are You the Christ, the Son of the Blessed One?' And Jesus said,*

'I am; and you shall see the Son of Man sitting at the right hand of power, and coming with the clouds of heaven.' Tearing his clothes, the high priest said, 'What further need do we have of witnesses? You have heard the blasphemy; how does it seem to you?' And they all condemned Him to be deserving of death."

The council is unable to fulfill the legal requirement of two witnesses to agree as to the charges against Jesus. The chief priest then resorts to efforts to get Jesus to incriminate Himself (which is also a violation of their law). Jesus finally cooperates by clearly declaring who He is in order to fulfill the prophecies regarding his execution for the sins of humanity and His resurrection proving both His identity and that His death was the sufficient atonement (Psalm 22; Isa. 53; Zech. 12:10). Jesus declares Himself to be the Messiah and the Son of God. The response of the Sanhedrin obviously indicates they know the statement of Jesus is a claim to be God.

Mark 15:38. "*And the veil of the temple was torn in two, from top to bottom.*" This veil separated the temple into the Holy of Holies into which only the high priest could go. Torn from top to bottom indicates first of all that it was not of human doing, and secondly was symbolic indicating that access into the presence of God was now available to any because Jesus' death had paid for sin once and for all.

The Gospel of Luke

Luke 1:17. Speaking of the son promised to Zacharias and Elizabeth, whom they are to name John, the angel of the Lord declares, "*And he will turn many of the sons of Israel back to the Lord their God. It is he who will go as a forerunner before him in the spirit and power of Elijah, to turn the hearts of the fathers back to the children, and the disobedient to the attitude of the righteous, so as to make ready a people prepared for the Lord.*"

Luke did research for writing this Gospel so there is more background information and more historical references than in the other gospels. It is obvious in this passage that John is to prepare the way for the appearing of the Lord God to the people of Israel. In addition, Luke refers to the promise God made in Malachi 3:1 about one being sent to prepare the way ahead for the arrival of God himself.

Luke also includes a reference to Malachi 4:5-6 where Elijah, restoration and the coming of the Lord are each mentioned as related to John's purpose. These verses introduce the fact that the one for whom John is preparing the way will be The Lord God.

Luke 1:31-32, 34-35. *"And behold, you will conceive in your womb and bear a son and you shall name Him Jesus. He will be great and will be called the Son of the Most High: and the Lord God will give Him the throne of His father David ...*[259] *Mary said to the angel, 'How can this be, since I am a virgin?' The angel answered and said to her, 'The Holy Spirit will come upon you, and the power of the Most High will overshadow you and for that reason the holy Child shall be called the Son of God.'"*

This affirms the virgin birth; that the birth of Jesus will not be the result human physical intimacy but of a supernatural act of God. The one to be born of this miraculous conception will thus, for that reason be called the Son of God.

Luke 1:42-43. Based upon the angel's words, Mary goes to visit her relative who is near to giving birth. *"And she cried out with a loud voice and said, 'Blessed are you among women, and blessed is the fruit of your womb! And how has it happened to me that the mother of my Lord would come to me?'"* In this passage Elizabeth acknowledges that the yet unborn baby of Mary is her Lord. The child to be born of Mary is thus presented in this acknowledgement as both God and man.

Luke 1:76. Zacharias speaking to and of his newborn son states, *"And you, child, will be called the prophet of the Most High; for you will go on before the Lord to prepare His ways."* This is another reference to the promise of Malachi 3:1 that God is coming to His people and will be preceded by one sent in advance to prepare His way. John, the son of Zacharias is to be that forerunner. Each of these occurrences in chapter one is presented as preparing the way for Jesus as the fulfillment of God coming to the people of Israel.

Luke 2:10-11. *"But the angel said to them, 'Do not be afraid; for behold, I bring you good news of great joy which will be for all the people; for today in the city of David there has been* born for you a Savior, who is Christ The Lord." This too indicates that Jesus is God. First of all because at Isaiah 43:11 God informs us that, "I, even I, am the Lord, and there is no savior besides Me." So, for Luke to call Jesus Savior in addition to calling Him Lord are both indications that He is God. Also see Luke 1:46-47.

Luke 3:21-22. "Now when all the people were baptized, Jesus was also baptized, and while He was praying, heaven was opened, and the Holy Spirit descended upon Him in bodily form like a dove and a voice came out of heaven, 'You are my beloved Son, in You I am well-pleased.'" Jesus is authenticated by the Holy Spirit descending upon Him and by the voice of the Father. The Trinity are each presented in this passage, Holy Spirit, Father, and Son.

Luke 5:20-25. Jesus speaks to them "Seeing their faith, He said 'Friend, your sins are forgiven you.' The scribes and Pharisees began to reason saying, 'Who is this man who speaks blasphemies? Who can forgive sins, but God alone?' But Jesus, aware of their reasonings, answered and said to them, 'Why are you reasoning in your hearts? Which is easier, to say, Your sins have been forgiven you, or to say, 'Get up and walk?' But, so that you may know that the Son of Man has authority on earth to forgive sins – He said to the paralytic – I say to you get up, and pick up your stretcher and go home.' Immediately he got up before them, and picked up what he had been lying on, and went home glorifying God."

It is possible that this is a similar occurrence to the one in Matthew 9. However, it is most likely a parallel account of the paralyzed man being brought to Jesus. Luke just adds more specific details than Matthew. Jesus claims the prerogative of God to be able to forgive sins and confirms that right by healing the man. As in the Mark account, the religious leaders are correct in their theological understanding that forgiveness of sin is God's prerogative, but unwilling to see that it is God among them who is declaring that forgiveness.

Luke 6:2, 5. "But some of the Pharisees said, 'Why are you doing what is not lawful on the Sabbath' … And he was saying to them, The Son of Man is Lord of the Sabbath." This a repetition of the claim Jesus made that He is in charge of the Sabbath which God instituted in Exodus 20. The Jews were continually reminded that they were to observe this day as a requirement established by God (Lev. 26:2; Duet. 5:12; Isaiah

58:13; Ezekiel 20:12). So, for Jesus to state He is Lord of the Sabbath is a clear declaration to be God.

Luke 7:13-16. Jesus, His disciples, and a large crowd approach the gate of the city of Nain as a dead man is being carried out. Another crowd from the city are accompanying the mother of the dead man. She is a widow. *"When the Lord saw her, He felt compassion for her, and said to her, 'Do not weep.' And He came up and touched the coffin; and the bearers came to a halt. And He said, 'Young man, I say to you, arise!' The dead man sat up and began to speak. And Jesus gave him back to his mother. Fear gripped them all, and they began glorifying God, saying 'A great prophet has arisen among us' and 'God has visited his people!'"*

Just as God spoke reality into existence at the beginning, and created all forms of life including humans, so Jesus is able to speak the words and restore life to the dead. Jesus' miracles were each done out of compassion for those who were suffering (Mark 1:41; 6:34; 8:1), in this case for the widowed mother. Jesus refused to perform a miracle merely to prove His Power (Matt. 4:2-4; 26:68; Mark 8:11-12; 15:29-32; Luke 23:8-11, 35-39).

Luke 7:27. *"This is the one about whom it is written, 'Behold I send my messenger ahead of You, who will prepare Your way before You.'"* This is another reference to Malachi 3:1, speaking of the forerunner promised to prepare the way for God to come to His people. Jesus is telling the people that John the Baptist was that forerunner or messenger. This indicates that Jesus is proclaiming Himself as God who has presented Himself.

Luke 7:48-50. *"Then He said to her, 'Your sins have been forgiven.' Those who were reclining at the table with Him began to say to themselves, 'Who is this man who even forgives sins?' And He said to the women, 'Your faith has saved you; go in peace.'"* This is an additional example of Jesus claiming that He, Himself has the divine right to forgive sin. This time adding that the women's faith in Him has resulted in her salvation.

Luke 8:24-25. *"They came to Jesus and woke Him up, saying 'Master, Master, we are perishing!' And He got up and rebuked the wind and the surging waves, and they stopped, and it became calm. And He said to them, 'Where is your faith?' They were fearful and amazed, saying to one another,*

'Who then is this, that he commands even the winds and the water, and they obey Him?'" This is another account of the events recorded in Matthew 8:26-27. Who has the power to control the forces of nature itself?

Luke 8:28, 31-32, 35, 39. Following are excerpts from this account of the healing and deliverance of the Gerasene man possessed by demons. *"Seeing Jesus, he cried out and fell before Him, and said in a loud voice, 'What business do we have with each other, Jesus, Son of the Most High God? I beg you do not torment me.' ... 'They were imploring Him not to command them to go away into the abyss. ... and implored Him to let them enter the swine and He gave them permission.' ... 'The people went out to see what had happened; and they came to Jesus, and found the man from whom the demons had gone out, sitting down at the feet of Jesus, clothed and in his right mind; and they became frightened.' ... 'Return to your house and describe what great things God has* done for you.' *So he went away, proclaiming throughout the whole city what great things Jesus had done for him."*

Notice that the demons recognized who Jesus was, were afraid of Him and acknowledge that He had authority over them. The passage also indicates that what had been accomplished for the man who had been possessed was done by God.

Luke 8:49-50, 52-55. *"While He was still speaking someone came from the house of the synagogue official, saying, 'Your daughter has died; do not trouble the Teacher anymore.' But when Jesus heard this, He answered him, 'Do not be afraid any longer; only believe, and she will be made well.' ... Now they were all weeping and lamenting for her; but He said, 'Stop weeping, for she has not died, but is asleep.' And they began laughing at Him, knowing that she had died. He, however, took her by the hand and called, saying, 'Child arise!' And her spirit returned, and she got up immediately, and He gave orders for something to be given her to eat. Her parents were amazed; but He instructed them to tell no one what had happened."*

This is the same incident recorded in Matthew 9. In this case, the synagogue official knew that Jesus could heal but he and his wife were amazed that Jesus actually brought their daughter back to life. Jesus instructs them not to tell anyone what had happened. This demonstrates that Jesus acts out of compassion; He does miracles to solve problems and meet people's needs, not to gain attention or wealth. (See: Matt 8:4; 9:30; Mark 1:44)

Luke 9:1-2. *"And He called the twelve together, and gave them power and authority over all the demons and to heal diseases. And He sent them out to proclaim the kingdom of God and to perform healing."*

This is another account of Jesus temporarily bestowing some of His power and authority upon His apostles in order for them to expel demons, to heal and to proclaim the kingdom of God. This is the bestowal by Jesus of some of the power and authority of God. How would they receive that power by Him merely telling them?

Luke 9:26. *"For whoever is ashamed of me and my words, the Son of Man will be ashamed of him when He comes in His glory, and the glory of the Father and of the holy angels."* Glory, in reference to God refers the awesomeness of who He is; to His greatness, His majesty, splendor, power and authority. Who is this Jesus, who claims he will return in His glory and glory of the Father and of the holy angels?[260]

Luke 9:34-35. "While he was saying this a cloud formed and began to overshadow them; and they were afraid as they entered the cloud. The voice came out of the cloud, saying, 'This is my Son, My Chosen One, Listen to Him.'" Peter was speaking nonsense, and God intervened and said listen to Jesus. The voice declares Jesus to be the Son of God and the Chosen One to provide the sin payment.

Luke 10:22. *"All things have been handed over to Me by My Father, and no one knows who the Son is except the Father, and who the Father is except the Son and anyone to whom the Son wills to reveal Him."* Jesus is claiming to have received the authority of God, including the authority to reveal God, the Father. He also states that no one actually knows God unless the Son of God reveals Him to them.

Luke 11:30. *"For just as Jonah became a sign to the Ninevites, so will the Son of Man be to this generation."*

Luke does not go on to explain how the prophet Jonah was a sign as Matthew did (Matt. 12:39-41). We know that Jonah's experience and mission somehow portrayed Jesus' mission and what Jesus was soon to experience in his death, burial, and resurrection. In the next two verses (31-32), Jesus declares that He is greater than Solomon and greater than Jonah.

Luke 12:8-9. *"And I say to you, everyone who confesses me before men, the Son of Man will confess him also before the angels of God; but he who denies me before men will be denied before the angels of God."*

Who is Jesus that He is of such importance that the acknowledgement or denial of Him before men is of such significance? What is it that is to be confessed before men?

Luke 12:40. *"You too, be ready; for the Son of Man is coming at an hour you do not expect."*

Jesus was with them at the time he told the parable and its application in verse 40. So, he was obviously referring to a future at which He would return. Who is He claiming to be to know He will come back and that His return would be unexpected?

Luke 13:34-35. *"O Jerusalem, Jerusalem, the city that kills the prophets and stones those sent to her! How often I wanted to gather your children together just as a hen gathers her brood under her wings, and you would not have it. Behold. Your house is left to you desolate; and I say to you, you will not see Me until the time comes when you will say, 'Blessed is He who comes in the name of the Lord'"*

This is an expression of the concern and loving compassion God has for His people Israel despite their continued rebellion and rejection of the prophets and of Him. He mentions the destruction to come to Jerusalem, and then refers to His return by quoting Psalm 118:26.

Luke 17:20-21. *"Now having been questioned by the Pharisees as to when the Kingdom of God was coming, He answered them and said, 'The kingdom of God is not coming with signs to be observed; nor will they say, 'Look, here it is!' or, 'There it is! For behold the kingdom of God is in your midst.'"*

Jesus was standing among them representing the kingdom of God since he is both God and King. Jesus was stating that the kingdom of God was present at that time in His own person as God and the king. See also Matt. 12:28.

Luke 18:31. "Then He took the twelve aside and said to them, 'Behold we are going up to Jerusalem, and all things which are written through the prophets about the Son of Man will be accomplished.'"

Jesus states that the prophets wrote about Him, and that He is fulfilling their prophecies. What were their predictions? Who is Jesus according to this assertion?

Luke 19:30-35. *"Go into the village ahead of you; there, as you enter, you will find a colt tied on which no one yet has ever sat; untie it and bring it here. If anyone asks you, 'Why are you untying it?' You shall say, 'The Lord has need of it.' So those who were sent went away and found it just as He had told them."*

In addition to the special knowledge of an animal in the village they have not yet arrived at, and the circumstances it would be found in, Jesus has referred to Himself as Lord.

Luke 21:13-15. *"It will lead to an opportunity for your testimony. So make up your minds not to prepare beforehand to defend yourselves; for I will give you utterance and wisdom which none of your opponents will be able to resist of refute."*

Jesus has been explaining to his disciples that in the future many will falsely claim to come in His name; that His followers will be persecuted, and has presented them with specific signs of the latter days. He adds that in the midst of these persecutions that He will supply the wisdom needed to answer opponents. How would it be possible for Him to give the needed response to His followers in future generations?

Luke 21:27. *"Then they will see the Son of Man coming in a cloud with power and great glory."*

Who is Jesus, that following all the conditions He has listed in regard to the future; He is to return to the earth in power and glory? There have been many who have claimed to be Jesus returned to the earth, including several in recent times. None of them have come in power and great glory, so they are all frauds.

Luke 21:33. *"Heaven and earth will pass away, but my words will not pass away."*

How does Jesus know that heaven and earth will be destroyed? Who would Jesus be if his words outlast this present physical universe? Luke repeats this statement of Jesus that also occurs in Matt. 24:35. See also Matt. 5:18; 7:24-29.

Luke 22:29-30. "… *and just as my Father has granted Me a kingdom, I grant you that you may eat and drink at My table in My kingdom, and you will sit on thrones judging the twelve tribes of Israel.*"

Who is this who confidently speaks about the future kingdom? Who is Jesus claiming to be that He can choose those who will judge the people of Israel? Who according to the Scriptures is the authority over the twelve tribes of Israel?

Luke 22:37. "*For I tell you that this which is written must be fulfilled in Me, 'And He was numbered with transgressors'; for that which refers to Me has its fulfillment.*"

Jesus again is asserting the Old Testament is about Him. He quotes from Isaiah 53 as referring to Himself as the guiltless sin bearer for humanity who would be unjustly executed along with actual criminals.

Luke 22:69-70. "'*But from now on the Son of Man will be seated at the right hand of the power of God' And they all said, 'Are You the Son of God then?' And He said to them, 'Yes I am.'*'"

Jesus is on trial before the Sanhedrin, the council of the religious leaders. These priests and scribes understood what Jesus words about Himself meant. They got Him to make a clear statement of His identity in front of the council in order to condemn Him for blasphemy.

Luke 24:25-27. "*And He said to them, 'O foolish men and slow of heart to believe in all that the prophets have spoken! Was it not necessary for the Christ to suffer these things and to enter into His glory?' Then beginning with Moses and with all the prophets, He explained to them the things concerning Himself in all the Scriptures.*"

Jesus informs the two He is walking with that all the Hebrew Scriptures (our Old Testament) are all about the Messiah. They do not realize that the One walking with them is that Messiah and Lord, resurrected from the dead until later when they prepare to eat and He blesses the food.

Luke 24:31-47. "Then their eyes were opened and they recognized Him; and He vanished from their sight. They said to one another, 'Were not our hearts burning within us while He was speaking to us on the road, while He was explaining the Scriptures to us?' And they got up that very hour and returned to Jerusalem, and found gathered together the eleven and those who were with them, saying, 'The Lord has really risen and has appeared to Simon'. They began to relate their experiences on the road and how He was recognized by them in the breaking of the bread. While they were telling these things, He Himself stood in their midst and said to them, 'Peace be to you'. But they were startled and frightened and thought that they were seeing a spirit.

"And He said to them, 'Why are you troubled, and why do doubts arise in your hearts? See My hands and My feet, that it is I Myself; touch Me and see, for a spirit does not have flesh and bones as you see that I have'. And when He had said this, He showed them His hands and his feet. While they still could not believe it because of their joy and amazement, He said to them, 'Have you anything here to eat?' They gave Him a piece of broiled fish; and He took it and ate it before them. Now He said to them, 'These are My words which I spoke to you while I was still with you, that all things which are written about Me in the Law of Moses and the Prophets and the Psalms must be fulfilled'. Then He opened their minds to understand the Scriptures, and He said to them, 'Thus is it written, that the Christ would suffer and rise again from the dead the third day, and that repentance for forgiveness of sins would be proclaimed in His name to all the nations, beginning from Jerusalem.'"

This long passage mentions Jesus' post resurrection appearance to Peter (Simon), to the two on the Emmaus Road and then to the eleven apostles plus those with them. It shows how difficult it was for Jesus disciples to realize He was really there, alive from the dead. He then explains, in verses 44-47 that the Old Testament Scriptures are about Him. For that to be true He must be not only the Messiah but God as well.

Luke 24:52. *"And they, after worshipping Him, returned to Jerusalem with great joy, and were continually in the temple praising God."*

First century Jews were strict monotheists. They would only worship someone they believed to be God.

Summary of the evidence from reading through the Synoptic Gospels

The purpose of this section of the book, has not been to prove the reliability of the Gospels, nor to prove that Jesus is divine. The purpose as mentioned at the start was to prove that each of the Synoptic Gospels present Jesus as being God. It can readily be seen by any objective reader, that each of the Synoptic Gospels presents Jesus to be both God and man. These passages in each of these gospels are not merely assertions that stand on their own but are cumulative evidence of what each writer intended for the readers to understand regarding the person of Jesus Christ.

In each of these biblical Gospels Jesus is presented as having demonstrated authority and power over disease, demons, the forces of nature and physical defects and injuries and even death itself (Luke 4:33-36; 4:38-41; 5:12-13; 5:23-26; 6:8-10; 7:13-15; 7:22; 8:24-25; 8:31-33; 9:12-17; 9:42; 11:20; 13:11, 13; 18:42; 22:51). These examples from Luke can be multiplied by those from Matthew and Mark. What conclusion would be reasonable to deduce from all these examples?

Jesus as portrayed in the Gospel of John

The Gospel of John, is assumed to be the last of the genuine gospels. John includes much additional in information that is not included in the other gospels. This should not be surprising as John was a member of Jesus' inner circle and the other gospel writers were not. Some of this additional information confirms that Jesus is God. Examples of this additional information is listed for the benefit of the reader.

John 1:1-5, 10, 12-14, 34; 3:13, 35-36; 4:25-26; 5:17-18, 22-27, 39, 46-47; 6:38-40, 62; 7:37-39; 8:56-58; 9:37-38; 10:28-31; 11:25-27; 12:44-46; 14:6,9; 17:1-5; 20:29, 31.

Interpolations or Deletions?

Many evangelicals have been taught to criticize and reject most modern translation of the New Testament because they allegedly delete or deny important biblical teachings. This is asserted in regard to the New American Standard, the New

112

International Version, etc. Usually, such teachings also include the exaltation of the King James Version as the most reliable. Such claims are however false. Though there are unreliable translations that mistranslate certain key passages in order to justify false teachings of cults,[261] that is not true of all modern translations.

In genuine translations, the supposed deletions are actually the elimination of interpolations. Interpolations are added words or verses later inserted into the original text during hand copying. These insertions were discovered by comparing the most ancient Greek manuscripts and quotations of the New Testament in other writings, in order to regain the original text.

Often the inserted words do appear as part of the genuine text elsewhere. In those cases, some later unknown writer sought to make the two passages say the same thing. This erroneous attempt to make two passages parallel ignored the differences in the original writer's vocabulary, purpose, and audience. The cross references show that the genuine occurrences of each of those teachings remain.

Another cause of interpolations occurred from someone writing a comment in the margin of the text in an attempt to explain something. John 5:3b-4 is an example of this. A later copyist, would often not know whether the added words were originally left out by the previous scribe or a later addition by someone else. Just to be safe he would usually include the additional words to ensure that nothing was being lost. So, the manuscript with the shorter text is almost always the authentic one.

Another type of example is that of Romans 8:1 in which a scribe must have accidently added a line from verse four *"who do not walk according to the flesh but according to the Spirit."* Eliminating these interpolations does not result in the loss or alteration of any genuine New Testament teaching! Verses added following the brackets indicates that the teaching does genuinely occur in other places within the New Testament.

Despite the concern of some conservative believers to the contrary, it is the King James Version that is less reliable. This is not only because we can eliminate these interpolations but also because we now possess more and older Hebrew manuscripts than were available in 1611. Also,

Hebrew is much better understood now than back then. We also possess older manuscripts of the Greek New Testament than were available in 1611. So, there are more reliable translations available now than the old KJV including the New American Standard, the New King James, the New International Version.

Critics sometimes try to make an issue out that the number of interpolations or variant readings of the biblical text. It is not actually the number that matters but what those interpolations actually add or alter. A number of examples of interpolations are listed below, mostly from the Gospels by book brackets that enclose each interpolation to show that they do not change or effect any important teaching in the New Testament. Read them along with your New Testament.

Matt. 6:13. [For yours is the kingdom and the power and the glory forever. Amen.]

Matt. 17:21. [But this kind does not go out except by prayer and fasting] See Mark 9:29.

Matt. 23:14. [Woe to you scribes and Pharisees, hypocrites, because you devour widows' houses and for a pretense you make long prayers; therefore, you will receive greater condemnation.] See Mark 12:40; Luke 20:47.

Mark 1:1. (possibly an interpolation) [the Son of God]

Mark 3:14. [whom he named apostles]

Mark 3:32. [and your sisters]

Mark 7:16. [If anyone has ears to hear, let him hear.]

Mark 7:24. [and Sidon]

Mark 9:29. [and fasting]

Mark 9:44, 46. [Where their worm does not die, and the fire is not quenched.] Repeated. See Mark 9:48; Isa. 66:24.

Mark 10:7. [shall cleave to his wife]

Mark 10:24. [for those who trust in wealth]

Mark 11:26. [But if you do not forgive, neither will your Father who is in heaven forgive you your Transgressions] See Matt. 6:15.

Mark 12:23. [when they rise again]

Mark 15:28. [And the Scripture was fulfilled which says, "And He was numbered with transgressors."]

Mark 16:9-20. It is believed that the original ending of Mark was lost. This ending and another one were added to some later manuscripts. Neither ending is considered authentic.

Luke 1:28. [you are blessed among women]

Luke 8:43. [who had spent all her living upon physicians]

Luke 8:45. [and those with him]

Luke 9:54-56. [As Elijah did ... and said, "You do not know what kind of spirit you are of; for the Son of Man did not come to destroy man's lives, but to save them]

Luke 11:2-4. [Our] Father ... [Your will be done on earth as it is in heaven] ... [but deliver us from the evil one] See Matthew 6:9-13.

Luke 11:11. [loaf, he will not give him a stone, will he, or for]

Luke 15:21. [make me as one of your hired men]

Luke 17:36. [Two men will be in the field; one will be taken and the other one left.] See Matthew 24:40.

Luke 23:17. [Now he was obliged to release to them at the feast one prisoner]

Luke 24:40. [and when He had said this, He showed them his hands and His feet]

Luke 24:51. [and was carried up into heaven]

Luke 24:52. [worshipped Him]

John 5:3-4. [waiting for the moving of the waters; for an angel of the Lord went down at certain seasons into the pool and stirred up the water; whoever then first after the stirring of the water, stepped in was made well from whatever disease with which he was afflicted.]

John 7:53-8:11. This well-known story of the woman caught in adultery sounds authentic, but is missing in some of the earliest manuscripts and occasionally appears elsewhere in the Gospels. It is thought to be an interpolation by many.

Some scholars assume this is a true event in the life of Jesus, but not part of the original New Testament Gospels.

Acts 8:37. [And Philip said, "If you believe with all your heart, you may" And he answered and said, "I believe that Jesus Christ is the Son of God."]

Acts 15:24. [you must be circumcised and keep the law.]

Acts 15:34. [But it seemed good to Silas to remain there.]

Acts 24:6b-8a. [We wanted to judge him according to our own law. But Lysias the commander came along and with much violence took him out of our hands, ordering his accusers to come before you.]

Acts 28:29. [When he had spoken these words, the Jews departed, having a great dispute among themselves.]

Rom.8:1. [who do not walk according to the flesh, but according to the Spirit]

Rom.16:24. [The grace of our Lord Jesus Christ be with you all. Amen.]

Ephesians 1:1. [at Ephesus]

1John 5:8. [in heaven, the Father, the word, and the Holy Spirit and these three are one. And there are three that bear witness on earth]

As you can see, the added words of these interpolations, with the exception of 1John 5:8, are quite insignificant. None of them were essential and their deletion does not alter any doctrine of the New Testament. See details on this 1John 5:8 interpolation at the end of the appendix on the Trinity.

English Translation from the Greek

There are also many other cases where additional words have been added in English that are not interpolations. This is because in translating from one language to another, frequently there is no one word that sufficiently or completely expresses the meaning of the other. In these cases, the extra words are necessary to fully express the meaning of the Greek word or are required to comply with English grammar.

The meaning is not altered in either of these cases and often the added English words can be dropped when reading that passage, showing the meaning is often clear either way. As you read these passages in their context you will see that no teaching if the New Testament is eliminated nor altered by the inclusion of elimination of the inserted words.

The Oxyrhynchrus papari are documents written from 6 to 104 A.D. which show that the New Testament writings were written in the Greek of the common people called Koine Greek. Those papyri also show parallels to the census reports in Luke and Acts.[262]

Appendix A: Early Non-Christian Sources About Jesus

Some atheists still pretend that there is no evidence Jesus ever lived even though there are secular and other non-Biblical references about him from the late first century on. A recent example of atheists ignoring the evidence occurred in September 2002. In Italy an atheist sued a Catholic priest for teaching that Jesus was an actual historical person. The suit was dismissed by the Appeals Court in Rome and the atheist fined for filing a fraudulent suit.[263]

In response to the Roman court's decision, the American Humanist's article suggested the court was discriminating against atheists. They chose that response rather than consider the actual evidence for or against Jesus' existence. The suggestion of discrimination was a convenient way to avoid dealing with the facts available which would have destroyed their pretenses.

In more recent example, Richard Dawkins in The God Delusion, published in 2006 wrote *"It is even possible to mount a serious, though not widely supported historical case that Jesus never lived at all."* (p. 122). It is true that such a case is not widely supported. It is not true that it is possible to mount a serious historical case that Jesus never lived, unless one is willing to ignore or deny the validity of history. As historian Paul Johnson wrote, *"the evidence of Jesus existence is abundant."*[264]

In addition to the specific historical documents that verify Jesus' existence, Johnson may have also been thinking of the movement Jesus instigated, which is the largest in history – the Christian Faith. It is impossible to realistically account for the origin of the Christian Faith without the person of Jesus, and His resurrection from the dead.

Dawkins goes on to admit that Jesus probably lived but that reputable Bible scholars don't regard the Old or New Testaments as reliable sources for what actually happened. By reputable scholars, he means those that agree with his perspective. There are many who are both reputable and convinced of the historical and textual reliability of the Biblical documents. Actually, there should be no doubt that Jesus existed. The New Testament Gospels are authentic, historical documents and the primary sources for Jesus' life, but there are other sources as well.

Field archaeologist and professor Titus Kennedy introduces his book on the archaeological evidence relating to Jesus with this sentence: *"Jesus of Nazareth is widely acknowledged as the most important and most famous figure in history, regardless of beliefs about God, religion, the Bible, Christianity or the church."*[265]

The earliest secular reference to Jesus that we know about is that of the Greek writer Thallus writing a history of the Mediterranean world about 52-57 A.D. He attributed the darkness at Jesus execution to a solar eclipse.[266] This is an acknowledgement of Jesus life, execution and the darkness that is said to have occurred in the middle of the day at His death.

The Jewish historian Josephus wrote of the Roman officials over Judea about 93 AD that "Possessed of such a character, Annas thought he had a favorable opportunity because *Festus was dead, and Albinus was still on the way. And so he convened the judges of the Sanhedrin and brought before them a man called James the brother of Jesus, who was called the Christ and certain others. He accused them of having transgressed the law and delivered them up to be stoned."*[267]

This refers to James, the leader of the church at Jerusalem being stoned to death during a gap in the presence of Roman prefects over Judea. Jesus is also mentioned off handedly. According to Josephus, Annas was removed from office for exceeding his authority by ordering this execution.[268]

Roman historian Cornelius Tacitus wrote in his acclaimed <u>Annuals</u> around 110-115 A.D. of the reign of Nero. Tacitus was a pagan historian who detested Christianity. Yet as he acknowledged a mere 31 years after the death of Jesus that there were *"a great number"* in Rome who believed so completely in Jesus that they gave their lives in Nero's persecution in 64 A.D. Historian Paul Maier wrote that *"For a philosophy or teaching to spread that far that fast is absolutely unparalleled in the ancient world, and historians have not devoted enough attention to the implications here."*[269]

Tacitus wrote that to suppress the rumor that he had started the fire that burned much of Rome, Nero *"falsely charged with the guilt, and punished with the most exquisite tortures, the persons commonly called Christians, who were hated for their enormities. Christus, the founder of that name, was put to death by Pontius Pilate procurator of Judea in the reign of Tiberius; but the pernicious superstition repressed for a time broke out again, not only through Judea, where the mischief originated but through the city of Rome also."* (<u>Annals</u> XV, 44).[270]

The 'pernicious superstition' is a reference to the Christians belief in Jesus as the Savior and Son of God and the teaching of Christ's resurrection from the dead. The Caesars were considered to be saviors and gods so any other claimant to such roles would be rejected by pagan officials and authors. The resurrection would have been considered a superstition by one not aware of the evidence supporting it as fact. The information Tacitus provides definitely confirms Jesus lived and his execution under Roman authority, as well as a few other details that confirm the New Testament records.[271]

Pliny the Younger, Governor of the Roman Province of Bithynia in Asia Minor wrote to the emperor Trajan (112 A.D.) for counsel regarding dealing with Christians. He explained he had been killing everyone discovered to be a Christian, men, women, and children. There were so many that he wondered if he should only kill certain ones.

Pliny stated in his letter of these Christians that, *"They affirmed, however that the whole of their guilt or error, was, that they were in the habit of meeting on a certain fixed day before it was light , when they sang in alternate verses a hymn to Christ as to a god, and bound themselves by a solemn oath, not to do any wicked deeds, but never to commit any fraud, theft, or adultery, never to falsify their word , not to deny any trust when they should be called upon to deliver it up."* (Epistle X, 96).[272]

Thus, Pliny informs us that these early Christians worshipped Christ as God and were committed to a high standard of moral and ethical behavior.

About 120 A.D. Roman historian and court official Suetonius wrote in his <u>Life of Claudius</u> (25, 4) of that emperor expelling the Jews from Rome. He wrote *"Since the Jews constantly made disturbances at the instigation of Chrestus, he expelled them from Rome."*[273] This was apparently controversy and conflict between Jews and Christians which is one of the earliest evidences of the Christian movement.

This confirms the expulsion that Luke refers to in Acts 18:2. In <u>The Lives of the Caesars,</u> Suetonius assumes Jesus was crucified in the early thirties and records that less than twenty years later Christians are in Rome. He mentions these Christians believed Jesus lived, died, and arose from the dead. Suetonius wrote of *"Punishment by Nero inflicted on the Christians a class of men given to a new and mischievous superstition."* (26, 2).[274]

Julius Africanus and Origen both mentioned, Phlegon who at around 140 A.D. wrote a history titled <u>Chronicles</u>. His writing referred to the solar eclipse and earthquake and prophecies of Jesus occurring during the reign of Tiberius Caesar.[275]

Lucian of Samosata, was a satirist who wrote scornfully of Christ and the early Christians approximately 170 A.D. in <u>The Passing of Peregrinus</u>. Peregrinus had been a cynic philosopher.

Lucian connected the Christians with the synagogues of Palestine and referred to Christ as *"... that other whom they still worship, the man who was crucified in Palestine because he introduced this new cult into the world ... furthermore their first lawgiver persuaded them that they were all brothers one of another after they have transgressed once for all by denying the Greek gods and by worshipping that crucified sophist himself and living under his laws."*[276]

Note that the Christian worship of Christ at the origin of Christianity is affirmed again as it was by Pliny. Lucian also confirms the crucifixion, Christians living by Christ's teachings, and rejection of the pagan gods.

Mara Bar-Serapion, a Syrian who was probably a stoic philosopher, refers to Jesus in a letter from prison to his son. This was written sometime after 73 A.D. and before 200 A.D. He encourages his son to pursue wisdom, and compares the unjust execution of Jesus to those of Socrates and Pythagorus. Not a Christian, he not only equates the three persons as equals but sees Jesus living on through his teachings rather than his resurrection.[277]

Galen of Pergamon (now Bergama, Turkey) was a Greek physician, writer, and philosopher. In Europe he exercised a dominant influence on medical theory and practice until the mid-17th century.[278] Approximately 180 AD he wrote, *"One might more easily teach novelties to the followers of Moses and Christ than to the physicians and philosophers who cling fast to their schools."* [279]

There are a couple of other possible early secular references to Jesus and several definitely in the Jewish Talmud substantiating his existence. One reference in the Talmud refers to Jesus being executed for enticing the Jews to apostasy. Another identifies Jesus and several of his disciples. A third item scoffs at the teaching Jesus was virgin born implying he was illegitimate.[280]

According to a former Roman polytheist Justin Martyr (100-165 A.D.), a Jewish writer named Trypho wrote that Jesus was executed for sorcery and attempting to seduce the Jewish people.[281] Martyr wrote a book in which he sought to refute Trypho's arguments.

These various references to Jesus, Talmudic as well as the secular ones are for the most part critical and unfriendly. These references are all unintentional verification of various facts about Jesus and early Christianity which makes them valuable and credible.

Those who deny or doubt that Jesus ever lived must ignore extensive early evidence that confronts their assumptions. The non-biblical sources confirm quite a few essential details about Jesus and early Christianity including that Jesus was worshipped. As F.F. Bruce wrote, *"The earliest propagators of Christianity welcomed the fullest examination of the credentials of their message."*[282]

The events that the Christian Faith is based upon were widely known and readily verifiable in the first century giving its advocates great confidence to welcome investigation. Christian believers continue to welcome objective evaluation of the origin and other evidences of our Faith.

Ralph Muncaster reminds us how amazing this amount of evidence is when you consider that about the years 30-60 A.D. very few writings are known to exist about anything.[283] He also stated that, *"To doubt the existence of Jesus is to doubt the reason for the largest movement in history."*[284]

<u>Appendix B</u>: Jesus' Fulfillment of Old Testament Prophecy

The following information is mainly condensed from material in Josh McDowell's excellent resource, <u>The New Evidence That Demands A Verdict</u>.[285] His book is highly recommended for a vast amount of evidence in support of the Christian faith and biblical Scriptures.

Using the argument that Jesus' fulfilling of Old Testament Scripture as evidence He is the promised Messiah began in the New Testament (Matt. 2:4-6; Acts 3:18; 10:43; 13:29; 17:2-3; 1Cor. 15:3-4).

Of the Old Testament Prophecies that Jesus fulfilled, some verify Him to be the promised Messiah; others indicate that He is also God. Jesus refers to prophecy being fulfilled by Him and through Him (Matt. 5:17; 26:24, 54; Luke 24:7). The prophecy reference(s) from the Old Testament are given first and followed by the reference(s) from the New Testament indicating the fulfillment by Jesus thus verifying that He is the promised Messiah.

The promise of God to send the Messiah, Dan. 9:25-26; Matt. 1:1; 16:16-17; John 1:41; 4:25-26.

Messiah to be the seed of a woman, Genesis 3:15; Galatians 4:4; Matt. 1:18-25.

Messiah to be virgin born, Isa. 7:14 (LXX "virgin")[286]; Matt. 1:18, 20-25; Luke 1:26-35.

From the linage of Abraham, Gen.12:2-3, 22:18; Matt. 1:1; Luke 3:34; Gal. 3:16.

Through the linage of Isaac, Gen. 21:12; Luke 3:23 & 34; Matt. 1:1-2.

Through linage of Jacob, Gen. 35:10-12; Num. 24:17-19; Luke 3:23 & 34; Matt. 1:2.

From tribe of Judah, Gen. 49:10; Micah 5:2; Luke 3:33; Matt. 1:2-3; Heb. 7:14.

Would be born of the family of Jesse, Isa. 11:1-10; Luke 3:32; Matt. 1:5-6.

Linage of David, 1Chron. 17:11-14; Jer. 23:5; Luke 3:31; Matt. 1:1; 9:27; 15:2; Acts 13:22-23.

He would be born in Bethlehem, Micah 5:2; Matt. 2:1, 5, 6, & 16; Luke 2:4-7; John 7:42.

An attempt made to kill him as an infant, Jer. 31:15; Matt. 2:16-18.

He would be brought back from Egypt, Hosea 11:1; Matt. 2:14-15.

To be worshipped & given gifts as a child, Psa. 72:10; Isa. 60:6; Matt. 2:11.

Existed prior to physical birth-- Isa. 9:6; Micah 5:2; John 1:1-3, 14 & 30; 8:58; 17:5; Col. 1:16-17; Heb. 1:2.

Be preceded by a messenger, Isa. 40:3; Mal. 3:1; 4:5; Matt. 3:1-3; 11:10; Luke 1:17; John 1:23.

Ministry to begin in Galilee, Isa 9:1; Matt. 4:12-13 & 17.

He would do miracles, Isa. 35:5-6; Matt. 11:4-6.

He would teach using parables Psa. 78:2; Matt. 13:34.

Would have a special anointing of the Holy Spirit, Psa. 45:7; Isa. 11:2; 61:1-2; Matt. 3:16-17; Luke 4:15-21; John 1:32.

Would be the Son of God--Psalm 2:7 & 12; 45:6-7; Isa. 9:6; 1Chr. 17:11-14; Matt. 3:17; 16:16-17; Luke 9:35; John 1:34, 49; Heb. 1:2-8.

Would be called Immanuel (God with us), Isa. 7:14; Matt. 1:23; Luke 7:16.

Would be known as the Son of Man--Daniel 7:13; Matt 8:20; 9:6; 11:19 (and many other examples).

Would be called Messiah (Christ) Daniel 9:25-26; Matt. 1:1, 16:16-17; Mark 8:29-30; John 1:41; 4:25-26.

Would be called Lord, Psa. 110:1; Jer. 23:5-6; Luke 2:11; Matt. 22:42-45; John 13:13.

Would be a Prophet, Deut. 18:15 &18; Matt. 21:11; Luke 7:16; John 4:19; 6:14; 7:40.

Would be a Priest, Psa. 110:4; Zech. 6:13; Heb. 3:1; 5:6; 6:20.

Born to be king, Psa. 2:6-7; Jer. 23:5-6; Zech. 9:9; Matt. 2:2 & 6; 21:5; John 12:12-15; 18:33-39.

Enter Jerusalem in apparent triumph on a donkey, Zechariah

9:9; Matt. 21:1-9; John 12:12-16.

Betrayed by a friend, Psa. 41:9; 55:12-14; Matt. 10:4; 26:49-50; John 13:18, 21-22.

Be betrayed for 30 pieces of silver, Zech. 11:12; Matt. 26:14-15; 27:3-4.

Betrayal money thrown into the temple, Zech. 11:13; Matt. 27:5.

Betrayal money bought the Potter's Field, Zech. 11:12-13; Matt. 27:7 & 10.

Be rejected by his people, Psa. 118:22; Isa. 53:3; Matt. 26:3-4; Luke 23:13-18, 21-23; John 1:11; 12:37; Acts 4:10-11.

He would be forsaken by disciples, Zech. 13:7; Isa. 53:4; Matt. 26:56; Mark 14:50.

He would be accused by false witnesses, Psa. 27:1; 35:11; Matt. 26:59-60; Mark 14:55-59.

He would remain silent before His accusers, Isa. 53:7; Matt. 26:62; 27:12-14; Mark 14:60-61; 15:4-5; Luke 23:9; Acts 8:32.

He would be tried and condemned, Isa. 53:8; Luke 23:1-25; Matt. 27:1-2, 11-26.

His conviction would be unjust, Isa. 53:7, 8; Matt. 26:59-60; Mark 15:9-15; Luke 23:13-24.

Be wounded, bruised, etc., Isa. 50:6; 52:14; 53:5; Matt. 27:29-30; Mark 14:65; 15:17-19.

Be hit, spit on, beard pulled out, Isa. 50:6; Matt. 26:67; 27:30; Mark 14:65; 15:19; Luke 22:63.

He would be mocked, insulted, Job 30:9-13; Psa. 22:7-8; Matt. 27:28-31, 39-44; Mark 15:17-20, 29-32; Luke 23:11, 35-37 & 39.

Be hated for no reason, Psa. 69:4; John 15:25.

Be executed by crucifixion, Psa. 22:14-17; Zech. 12:10; Mark 15:15 & 24-25; Luke 23:20-24; John 19:16.

Be executed with criminals, Isa. 53:9 & 12; Matt. 27:38; Luke 23:32-33.

To be given vinegar & gall to drink, Psa. 69:21; Matt. 27:34; Mark 15:23 & 36; John 19:28-30.

His executioners would divide His clothes among them, Psa.

22:18; John 19:23-24.

Observers of execution would shake their head at Jesus, Psa. 22:7; 109:23; Matt. 27:39.

His bones would not be broken, Ex. 12:46; Numbers 9:12; John 19:31-36.

He would die for mankind's sins, Isa. 53:5-12; Mark 10:45; John 1:29; 11:49-52; Acts 4:12; 10:43; 1Peter 2:24-25.

He would pray for His persecutors, Isa. 53:12; Luke 23:34.

He would commit Himself to God, Psa. 31:5; Luke 23:46.

Darkness would occur at midday, Amos 8:9; Matt. 27:45.

He would be buried in a rich man's tomb, Isa. 53:9; Matt. 27:57-60.

He would be Resurrected, Psa. 16:9-11; 49:15; Isa. 53:11-12; Matt. 28; Mark 16:1-8; Luke 24; Acts 1:3; 2:30-31; 13:35-37.

That He would ascend to heaven, Psa. 68:18; Acts 1:9.

In regard to all these fulfillments Norman Geisler stated,

"All of these supernatural prophecies were uniquely fulfilled in Jesus Christ. This is not true of any great religious leader or person who ever lived, including Muhammad."[287]

It is true that a few of these fulfillments of prophecy were the result of the deliberate actions of Jesus. It is evident, however, to anyone paying serious attention to the Gospels, that many fulfillments were outside of Jesus control. The possibility that all of these fulfillments of prophecy being merely coincidence or the result of deliberate efforts is completely irrational. It is important also to remember that the Gospel writers and preachers would not have been willing to die for something they made up.

Appendix C: Jesus Is God

How the Old Testament and the New Testament show that Yahweh, God the Father, and the Messiah, Jesus, the Son are both God, possessing the same characteristics, nature, and roles. The Old Testament references are given first and the New Testament references follow:

God is the Creator in the Old Testament: Gen. 1:1; Isa. 40:28. Jesus is presented as the Creator in the New Testament: John 1:1-3; Col. 1:15-16; Heb. 1:1-2.

God is the Judge: Psa. 50:1-6; Isa. 13:9-11. Jesus is the Judge: Jn. 5:22-27; 2Thess. 1:7-8.

God is the Healer: Ex. 15:26; Psa. 35:2, 5. Jesus is the Healer: Matt. 8:3, 13-17; Lk. 7:22.

God is Lord of the Sabbath: Ex. 16:23, 29; Lev. 19:3. Jesus is Lord of the Sabbath: Matt. 12:2-8; Mark 2:28.

God commands the sea: Psa. 89:8-9. Jesus commands the sea: Matt. 14:24; Mk. 4:37-39.

God knows our thoughts: Job 42:1-2; 1Chron. 28:9. Jesus knows our thoughts: Lk. 5:22; 11:16-17; Jn. 1:47-49.

God will feed His people: Psa. 132:13-15. Jesus fed the people: Matt. 14:19-20.

God accepts acclamation as God: Isa. 43:12. Jesus accepts acclamation as God: Jn. 20:27-29.

God accepts worship: Ex. 34:14; Matt. 4:10. Jesus accepts worship: Matt. 14:33; 28:9 & 17; Lk. 24:51-55; Jn. 9:38.

God forgives sin: Psa. 32:5; Isa. 43:16 & 25. Jesus forgives sin: Mk. 2:5-11; Lk. 5:20-23; 7:47-48.

A forerunner will prepare the way for God to come to His people: Isa. 40:3; Mal. 3:1. A forerunner came to prepare the way for Jesus: Matt. 3:3; Lk. 1:76; 3:4.

God would be a stumbling stone to Israel: Isa. 8:13-14. Jesus became a stumbling stone to Israel: 1Pet. 2:7-8.

God is the Shepherd of His people: Psa. 23 & 80:1, Ez. 34:30-31. Jesus is the shepherd: Jn. 10:11-16; 1Pet. 2:24-25.

God is called the Savior, and there is no other: Isa. 43:11; 45:21. Jesus is the Savior: Lk. 2:11; Acts 4:12; 2Pet. 1:11. In Titus 1:3-4 both God and Jesus are called Savior. This occurs again in Titus 2:10 & 13.

Salvation through His name: Joel 2:32. Salvation through Jesus' name: Rom. 10:9-10.

God is light: Psa. 27:1; Jn. 1:5. Jesus is the light: Jn. 8:12; 9:5.

God is our righteousness: Jer. 23:5-6. Jesus is our righteousness: 1Cor. 1:30; 2Cor. 5:21.

Every knee will bow to God: Isa. 45:23; Rom. 14:11. Every knee will bow to Jesus: Phil. 2:9-10.

God is the 'first and the last': Isa. 41:4; 48:12. Jesus the 'first and the last': Rev. 1:8; 22:12-16.

God won't share His glory with another: Isa. 42:8. Jesus shared glory with God: Jn. 1:14; 17:5.

God is the king over all the earth: Zech. 14:9; 1Tim. 6:15-16. Jesus will be the king over all the earth: Rev. 19:12.

God revealed Himself as "I Am", the Eternally Self-Existent One: Ex. 3:13; Isa. 43:13. Jesus revealed Himself as "I Am", the eternally self-existent one: Jn. 8:52-59. See also Col. 1:17; Heb. 13:8.

The above Appendix C material is revised & expanded from: C.H. Brown. Jesus Is Jehovah, Ralph E. Welch Foundation, 1963.

Appendix D: Evidence for the Resurrection

The resurrection of Jesus Christ is not merely an important teaching of the Christian faith—it is the central core of Christianity. The resurrection relates to and verifies every aspect of the faith. This is only a brief summary of the evidence for the literal, physical resurrection of Jesus Christ from the dead. See my book <u>Is Jesus Christ Alive?</u> for an extended presentation of that evidence. For Old Testament prophecies of the resurrection of the Messiah see the list in Appendix A.

As mentioned earlier, the claim that the church hid or destroyed evidence disproving the resurrection has no merit. There would never have been a church without the first century disciples becoming completely convinced from the evidence that the resurrection had occurred. In addition, without the certainty of the resurrection the New Testament would never have been written. The following will present some of the facts that show why that evidence was so compelling to them.

First is the empty tomb and that no one could find the body of Jesus. Related to the empty tomb is the second fact of the obvious appearances of Jesus. His appearances were unexpected, occurred at different times of the day and night to various groups of people. Jesus walks with disciples, is touched by them, eats in front of them, cooks them breakfast and continues teaching them. None of the skeptics' attempts to explain away these appearances as wishful thinking, hallucinations, mistaken identity etc. can account for all the information available.

Then you have the dramatic transformation of the apostles. They were terrified of receiving the same fate as Jesus and in hiding. Then suddenly they confront the religious leaders who could cause their executions and charged them as having caused the death of Jesus. They risked death, and many of them were killed for proclaiming the resurrection and eternal life only came through faith in Jesus. Many people have died for lies they thought were the truth, but no one is willing to die for something they know to be a lie. That proves the disciples did not make up the story of the resurrection, because they were willing to die for what they taught. They were obviously genuinely convinced that Jesus was alive!

Following the resurrection Jesus did not appear only to his followers. He appeared to his unbelieving half-brother James who later became the leader of the church. There is also the conversion of the Pharisee, Saul, a hostile enemy of Jesus followers. Saul was determined to destroy this threat to orthodox Judaism until Jesus confronted him and completely transformed him into the fervent apostle Paul declaring Jesus was alive.

Appendix E: The Biblical teaching of the Trinity

In a recent internet article, it was stated that Christianity should get rid of the teaching of the Trinity because it is crazy. The Pseudo-Christian cults deny that the Bible teaches that God is a Trinity or Triune. A major cause of this issue is that many people expect that they should be able to completely understand and accept anything that is true about God. What the skeptics would have us do is to eliminate anything about God that does not agree with their own thinking.

Doing so would turn Christianity into another merely human religion and God into the image of man. The cult of theological Liberalism has already done that and has departed from Christianity in everything essential but the name. The finite mind of man cannot fully comprehend the infinite Creator God. Neither are we free to change what God has revealed about Himself that may be difficult or impossible for us to comprehend. This teaching of the Christian faith is also attacked because it is a major example of the uniqueness of the Christian faith.

Thomas Paine thought he disposed of the concept of the Trinity by merely claiming it was a reduction from the number of pagan gods to three with no basis except his own declaration. However, this teaching has no relationship to pagan concepts or numbers, nor is it regarding three gods.

Proof the Trinity is a New Testament Teaching

One of the many ways that Christianity is fundamentally different from the world religions is its conception of God. Examples are that YAHWEH is both transcendent & Immanent. Transcendent means God exists prior to and outside of His creation. Immanent means that he is also involved within His Creation. He is also infinite, and personal, and is both everywhere present and yet focused in one place in the body of Jesus Christ. Another major uniqueness of the Biblical Christian concept of God is His being Triune. Christianity teaches that while there is only one true God, He exists as three personalities or persons within that oneness. God exists as a Trinity.

This is an essential element of genuine Christianity. As Robert Brow stated in Religion: Origins and Ideas, "The *doctrine of the Trinity is connected with every branch of theology, and it makes Christian theology absolutely different from the theology of every other religion or sect.*"[288]

Skeptics, liberal theologians, as well as the other cults and religions, deny the Trinity because they want a religion and a God who is completely comprehensible to man. In addition, they want to eliminate a major component of the uniqueness of the Christian faith.

It is completely irrational to think that the complete truth about God would be fully comprehended by humans. There is no possibility that an infinite God could be completely comprehended by a finite mind. The God who is capable of creating this vast universe and the amazing variety of living things is so far beyond our comprehensions that we could know nothing of Him except through his revelation of Himself to us.[289]

The doctrine of the Trinity is not merely using three different names for the same person nor a belief in three separate Gods. Neither is it merely referring to three modes of operation of the same person. The primary text proving this concept is usually that of Matthew 28:19 "*Go therefore and make disciples of all the nations baptizing them in the name of the Father, and the Son and the Holy Spirit ...*" Not only does the verse require that the three persons are equal as God, but the word translated 'name' is singular further suggesting the unity or oneness of the three.

There are many other references which clearly demonstrate the Triune nature of God. Two very key or primary examples follow: "*The grace of the Lord Jesus Christ, and the love of God and the fellowship of the Holy Spirit be with you all.*" 2Corinthians 13:14. "*But when the kindness of God our Savior and His love for mankind appeared, He saved us, not on the basis of deeds we have done in righteousness, but according to his mercy, by the washing of regeneration and renewing by the Holy Spirit, whom He poured out upon us richly through Jesus Christ our Savior, ...*" Titus 3:4-6

There are also verses that prove the Holy Spirit is not merely the influence or active power of the Father but is an actual individual, a Person of the Triune God. Jesus states in John 14:16-17, "I will ask the Father, and He will give another Helper, that He may be with you forever; that is the Spirit of truth, Whom the world cannot receive, because it does not see Him or know Him, but you know Him because He abides with you and will be in you."

John 14:26 repeats, *"But the Helper, the Holy Spirit whom the Father will send in My name, He will teach you all things and bring to your remembrance all that I said to you."* See also John 15:26 and 16:7-15. This Helper is repeatedly referred to as "He", is being sent by the Father and said to teach the disciples, be a witness to Christ and *"He shall glorify me,"* etc.

The teaching of the Trinity is a central and foundational teaching of the New Testament. Any individual or group that denies the Trinity is likely to deny other major teachings of the New Testament as well.

An extensive list follows of references revealing the reality and centrality of the Trinity in the New Testament and therefore the centrality of this doctrine to the Christian faith. As you will see, every New Testament writer shows the reality of the Triune nature of God.

This section goes into detail to list places where the names and titles of the triune God are specified in close proximity. Read these passages in their complete context and it will be obvious they are not merely several names for the same person, but these passages all reveal the Triune nature of God.

Matthew 1:18-23 (Jesus Christ, Holy Spirit, Son, Jesus, Lord, God with us); 3:16-17 (Jesus, Spirit of God, voice from heaven, Son); 4:1-4 (Jesus, Spirit, Son of God, God); 12:28-32 (Spirit of God, God, Spirit, Son of Man); 22:41-45 (Jesus, Christ, the Spirit. Lord, Lord); 28:18-19 (Jesus, Father, Son, Holy Spirit).

Mark 1:9-12 (Jesus, the Spirit, voice from heaven, Son, the Spirit); 12:35-37 (Jesus, Christ, Holy Spirit, Lord, Lord).

Luke 1:30-35 (Jesus, Lord God, Son of the Most High, Holy Spirit, Son of God); 1:41-47 (Holy Spirit, Lord, Lord, God); 1:67-78 (Holy Spirit, Lord God, Most High, Lord, God); 2:25-30 (Holy Spirit, Lord's Christ, God); 3:21-22 (Holy Spirit, voice from heaven, My Son); 4:1-8 (Holy Spirit, Son of God, Lord your God); 4:9-14 (Son of God, Lord your God, Spirit); 10:21-22 (He [Jesus], Holy Spirit, Father, Father, Son, Father, Son); 12:8-10 (Son of Man, God, Holy Spirit).

John 1:32-34 (He, the Spirit, Holy Spirit, Son of God); 3:34-36 (God, Spirit, Father, Son); 6:62-69 (Son of Man, the Spirit, Father, Holy One of God); 14:13-17 (Father, Son, Helper, Spirit of truth); 14:23-26 (Father, We, Helper, Holy Spirit, Father, My name, He, I); 15:26 (Helper, I, Father, Spirit of truth father, Me); 16:5-8 (I, Him, Helper, Him, He, I, Father, Me); 16:13-15 (He, Spirit of truth, He, Me); 20:21-22 (Father, Me, I, Holy Spirit).

Acts 1:1-5 (Jesus, Holy Spirit, God, Father, Holy Spirit); 1:6-8 (Lord, Father, Holy Spirit, My); 2:31-33 (Christ, God, Father, Holy Spirit); 2:36-39 (God, Lord, Christ, Jesus Christ, Holy Spirit, Lord our God); 4:8-10 (Holy Spirit, Jesus Christ, God); 4:24-26 (God, Lord, Holy Spirit, Lord, Christ); 5:29-32 (God, Jesus, Savior, Holy Spirit, God); 7:55-56 (Holy Spirit, God, Jesus, Son of Man, God); 8:14-17 (God, Holy Spirit, Lord Jesus, Holy Spirit); 9:15-20 (Lord, Lord Jesus, Holy Spirit, Jesus, Son of God); 9:31-34 (Lord, Holy Spirit, Jesus Christ, Lord); 10:34-38 (God, Jesus Christ-Lord of all, God, Holy Spirit); 10:42-48 (He [God], One [Jesus], Holy Spirit, God, Holy Spirit, Jesus Christ); 11:15-17 (Holy Spirit, Lord, Holy Spirit, God, Lord Jesus Christ, God); 11:20-24 (Lord Jesus, Lord, God, Holy Spirit, Lord); 13:33-52 (Jesus, Son, Holy One, God, Lord, Holy Spirit); 15:8-11 (God, Holy Spirit, God, Lord Jesus); 15:19-28 (God, Lord Jesus Christ, Holy Spirit); 16:6-10 (Holy Spirit, Spirit of Jesus, God); 19:2-8 (Holy Spirit, Jesus, Lord Jesus Holy spirit, God); 20:21-24 (God, Lord Jesus Christ, Holy Spirit, Lord Jesus, God); 20:27-35 (God, Holy Spirit, God, Lord Jesus); 28:23-31 (God, Jesus, Holy Spirit, God, Lord Jesus Christ).

Romans 1:1-7 (Christ Jesus, God, Son, Son of God, Spirit of holiness, Jesus Christ our Lord, God our Father, Lord Jesus Christ); 5:1-11 (God, Lord Jesus Christ, Holy Spirit, Christ, God, Son, Lord Jesus Christ); 8:1-5 (Christ Jesus, God, Son, the Spirit); 8:9-11 (the Spirit, Spirit of God, Spirit of Christ, Christ, Christ Jesus, He [God], Spirit); 8:14-17 (Spirit of God, God, Father, the Spirit Himself, God, Christ) 8:26-39 (the Spirit, God, Son, God ,Son, He [Spirit], God, Christ Jesus, God, Christ Jesus our Lord); 9:1-5 (Christ, Holy Spirit, Christ, God); 14:17-18 (God, Holy Spirit, Christ); 15:7-13 (Christ, God, Holy Spirit); 15:16-19 (Christ Jesus, God, Holy Spirit, Christ Jesus, God, the Spirit, Christ); 15:30 (Lord Jesus Christ, the Spirit, God).

1Corinthians 2:2-5 (Jesus Christ, the Spirit, God); 2:8-16 (Lord of glory, God, the Spirit, God, the Spirit of God, the
134

Spirit from God, God, the Spirit, Spirit of God, Lord, Christ); 3:3-6 (Christ, God, Christ, God); 3:11-17 (Jesus Christ, God, Spirit of God, God); 6:10-11 (God, Lord Jesus Christ, the Spirit of God); 6:15-20 (Christ, Holy Spirit, God); 12:3-5 (Spirit of God, Jesus is Lord, Holy Spirit, Spirit, Lord, God); 12:7-18 (the Spirit, Christ, God);

2Corinthians 1:18-23 (God, Son of God, Christ Jesus, God, Christ, the Spirit, God); 3:4-8 (Christ, God, Christ, God, the Spirit, the Spirit); 3:14-18 (Christ, Lord, Spirit, Spirit of the Lord, Lord, the Spirit); 5:5-11 (God, Spirit, Lord, Christ, Lord, God); 13:14 (Lord Jesus Christ, God, Holy Spirit).

Galatians 2:20-3:5 (Christ, Son of God, God, the Spirit); 3:11-14 (God, Christ, Christ Jesus, the Spirit); 4:4-7 (God, His Son, the Spirit, Father, God); 5:16-25 (the Spirit, God, the Spirit, Christ Jesus, the Spirit); 6:7-12 (God, the Spirit, Christ, Lord Jesus Christ).

Ephesians 1:11-17 (Him [Father], Christ, Holy Spirit, God, Lord Jesus, God, Lord Jesus Christ, the Father); 2:13-22 (Christ Jesus, Christ, God, Spirit, Father, God, Christ Jesus, Lord, God, the Spirit); 3:4-7 (Christ, the Spirit, Christ Jesus, God); 3:11-17 (Christ Jesus our Lord, Father, His Spirit, Christ); 4:1-13 (Lord, the Spirit, Spirit, Lord, God and Father, Christ, Son of God, Christ); 4:30-32 (the Holy Spirit of God, God, Christ); 5:17-21 (Lord, the Spirit, Lord, Lord Jesus Christ, God, the Father Christ); 6:17-24 (the Spirit, God, the Spirit, Lord, God the Father, Lord Jesus Christ).

Philippians 2:1-11 (Christ, Spirit, God, Jesus Christ is Lord, God the Father); 2:27-3:3 (God, Lord, Christ, Lord, Spirit of God, Christ Jesus).

Colossians 1:1-8 (Jesus Christ, God, Father, Lord Jesus Christ, God, the Spirit); 1:9-15 (His-Spirit, Lord, God, Father, Son, God).

1Thessalonians 1:2-5 (God, Lord Jesus Christ, God, Father Holy Spirit); 1:6-10 (Lord, Holy Spirit, Lord, God, His Son); 4:1-8 (Lord Jesus, God, Lord, God, Holy Spirit); 5:18-23 (God, Christ Jesus, the Spirit, God, Lord Jesus Christ).

2Thessalonians 2:13-14 (God, Lord, the Spirit, Lord Jesus Christ).

1Timothy 2:13-16 (Christ Jesus, God, He [Jesus], the Spirit); 4:1-6 (the Spirit, God, Christ Jesus).

2Timothy 1:7-14 (God, Lord, Christ Jesus, Savior Christ Jesus, Holy Spirit).

Titus 3:4-8 (God our Savior, Holy Spirit, Jesus Christ our Savior, God).

Hebrews 2:3-9 (Lord, God, Holy Spirit, son of man); 3:4-7 (God, Christ, Son, Holy Spirit); 6:1-6 (Christ, God, Holy Spirit, God, Son of God); 9:8-14 (Holy Spirit, Christ, eternal Spirit, God); 10:10-15 (Jesus Christ, God, Holy Spirit); 10:29-31 (Son of God, the Spirit, Lord, God).

1Peter 1:1-3 (Jesus Christ, God the Father, the Spirit, God and Father, Lord Jesus Christ); 1:11-21 (Spirit of Christ, Christ, Holy Spirit, Jesus Christ, Holy One, Father, Christ, God); 2:15-21 (Christ as Lord, God, the Spirit, God, Jesus Christ); 4:11-16 (God, Jesus Christ, Christ, the Spirit, God).

2Peter 1:17-21 (God the Father, Son, Holy Spirit, God).

1John 3:21-24 (God, Son Jesus Christ, the Spirit); 4:2 (Spirit of God, Jesus Christ, God); 4:9-14 (God, Son, His Spirit, Father, Son, Jesus, Son of God); 5:5-10 (Jesus, Son of God, the Spirit, God, Son, Son of God, His Son).

Jude 19-21 (the Spirit, Holy Spirit, God, Lord Jesus Christ).

Revelation 1:4-10 (Jesus Christ, God and Father, Lord God, the Spirit, Lord); 2:7-11 (the Spirit, God, who was dead and has come to life [Jesus], the Spirit); 2:17-29 (the Spirit, Son of God, My Father, the Spirit); 3:5-6 (I [Jesus], My Father, the Spirit); 3:12-13 (I [Jesus], God, the Spirit); 3:21-22 (I [Jesus], My Father, the Spirit); 14:10-13 (God, the Lamb, God, Jesus, the Spirit); 21:6-10 (Alpha and Omega, God, the Lamb, the Spirit, God); 22:16-21 (I [Jesus], the Spirit, God, Lord Jesus).

- The passage in 1John 5:5-10 does reveal the teaching of the Trinity. The King James Version, however, includes additional words besides those listed above. These were added to that passage on the basis of very late manuscripts that sought to further strengthen the teaching of the Trinity. However, textual criticism has determined the additional words, not appearing in any of the older manuscripts, was therefore an interpolation, not part of the original text and has therefore been either noted as not in the earliest manuscripts or been excluded from accurate modern translations.

- Examples: the <u>New American Standard</u> excludes the added words from the text but shows them in a note explaining they are in a few late manuscripts. <u>The Revised Standard Version</u> excluded the additional words with no explanation. <u>The New Living Translation</u> excludes the additional words in the text with a footnote stating that a few very late manuscripts add them. <u>The New King James</u> includes the words with a footnote acknowledging that only a few very late manuscripts have them. <u>The Berkeley Version</u> on page 265 has a footnote stating: *"As true as the insertion is, of Father, Word, and Holy Spirit, it is not needed; for such is the clear teaching of the whole New Testament."*

The terms Lord and God at times are used of different members of the Trinity. Some may try to pretend that the various designations of Deity are all merely references to God, the Father. However, the clear designations of the three distinct members of the Godhead in the primary passages listed at the beginning of this appendix make it clear that the various terms are not merely synonyms for one personality. but three. It should be obvious that the Triune nature of God is an essential teaching that permeates the New Testament.

To use an argument stated by someone previously, to read the New Testament and not see the teaching of the Triune nature of God presented there would be like that person looking at a cloudless sky at midday and not seeing the sun.

Appendix F: The New Testament Use of the Old Testament

The Hebrew Scriptures were the first scriptures of the infant church. However, the apostles saw that certain features or practices of those Scriptures were no longer necessary or valid. This was because they had been superseded or fulfilled in the person or the atoning work of Jesus Christ. Jesus had stated that He had come to fulfill the Law and the Prophets (Matt. 5:17), and to establish something new, the Church (Matt. 9:16-17; 16:18). So those things that were superseded or fulfilled were not to be part of this new covenant or new entity (See: Heb. 7:22, 27; 8:6-13). There were also to be new elements to the new covenant.

However, those prior Scriptures retained their significance as the preparation for the church and the new Scriptures as they began to be written and disseminated among the churches. The necessity of the Old Testament becomes apparent because without them we would be missing the first two thirds of the story. These earlier Scriptures were still necessary because they presented the origins of all things, the prophecies concerning God's plans, God's promises, and the person of the Christ. The extensive list to follow demonstrates the New Testament dependence upon the Old as the preparation for both the New Testament and the Church that grew out of the apostles' teachings.

The Gospel of Matthew, written especially to appeal to the Jewish people and benefit Jewish believers, uses the Old Testament extensively to show the continuity with these prior Scriptures and demonstrate how Jesus fit the promises given of God's Messiah. Matthew serves as sort of a transition between the Old and New Testaments.

Matthew chapter 1 - The legal Genealogy of Jesus

Matt. 1:2	Abraham – Gen. 11:28; 12:1-3; 17:19
	Isaac – Gen. 21:1-3
	Jacob – Gen. 25:26
Matt. 1:3	Perez – Gen. 46:12; 1Chron. 2:4
	Hezron – Ruth 4:18; 1Chron. 2:5
	Ram – Ruth 4:19; 1Chron. 2:9
Matt. 1:4	Amminadab – Ruth 4:19; 1Chron. 2:10
	Nahahon – Ruth 4:20; 1Chron. 2:10
	Salmon – Ruth 4:20; 1Chron. 2:11
Matt. 1:5	Boaz – Ruth 4:21; 1Chron. 2:11
	Obed – Ruth 4:21; 1Chron. 2:12
	Jesse – Ruth 4:22; 1Chron. 2:12
Matt. 1:6	David – Ruth 4:22; 1Chron. 2:15
	Solomon – 2Samuel 12:24; 1Chon. 3:5
Matt. 1:7	Rehoboam – 1Chron 3:10
	Abijah – 1Chron. 3:10
	Asa – 1Chron. 3:10
Matt. 1:8	Jehoshaphat – 1Chron. 3:10
	Joram/Jehoram – 1Chron. 3:11
	Uzziah – 1Chron. 3:11
Matt. 1:9	Jotham – 1Chron. 3:12
	Ahaz – 1Chron. 3:13
	Hezekiah – 1Chron. 3:13
Matt. 1:10	Manasseh – 1Chron. 3:13
	Amon/Amos – 1Chon 3:14
	Josiah – 1Chron. 3:14
Matt. 1:11	Jeconiah – 1Chron. 3:16
	Deportation to Babylon, 2Kings 24:12-16

Matt 1:12	Shealtiel – 1Chron. 3:17
	Zerubbabel – 1Chron. 3:19
Matt. 1:17	Abraham, David, deportation to Babylon
Matt. 1:20	Joseph's son (descendent) of David
Matt. 1:23	Quote from Isa. 7:14
Matt. 2:2	King of the Jews – Psa. 2:6; Jer. 23:5
Matt. 2:4-6	Messiah's birthplace – Micah 5:2
Matt 2:15	Son called out of Egypt – Hos. 11:1
Matt. 2:18	Children slain – Jer. 31:15
Matt. 3:3	A voice preparing the way for the Lord – Isa. 40:3
Matt. 3:9	Abraham
Matt. 4:4	Jesus quotes Deut. 8:3
Matt. 4:6	The devil quotes Psa. 91:11-12
Matt. 4:7	Jesus quotes Deut. 6:16
Matt. 4:10	Jesus quotes Deut. 6:13
Matt. 4:15-16	Quote from Isa. 9:1-2
Matt. 5:4	Reference to Isa. 61:2
Matt. 5:5	Reference to Psa. 37:11
Matt. 5:8	Reference to Psa. 24:3-4; 73:1
Matt. 5:12	Persecuted Prophets – 2Chron. 36:16
Matt. 5:17	Jesus to fulfill the Law & Prophets
Matt. 5:18	The smallest letter of the Law
Matt. 5:19	The least of the commandments
Matt. 5:21	You shall not commit murder – Ex. 20:13; Deut. 5:17
Matt. 5:27	You shall not commit adultery – Ex. 20:14; Deut. 5:18
Matt. 5:31	Give a certificate of divorce – Deut. 24:1, 3

Matt. 5:33	Fulfill your vows to the Lord – Num. 30:2; Deut. 32:21
Matt. 5:34-35	Throne & footstool of God – Isa. 66:1
Matt. 5:38	Eye for eye, tooth for tooth – Ex. 21:24; Lev. 24:20
Matt. 6:29	Solomon
Matt. 7:12	The Law & the prophets
Matt. 7:15	False prophets like ravenous wolves – Ezek. 22:25-28
Matt. 7:23	Quote Psa. 6:8
Matt. 8:4	Offering prescribed by Moses
Matt. 8:11	Abraham, Isaac & Jacob
Matt. 8:17	Quote from Isa. 53:4
Matt. 8:20	Calls Himself Son of Man – Psalm 80:17; Dan 7:13
Matt. 9:13	Quote from Hosea 6:6
Matt. 9:36	Like sheep without a shepherd – Ezek. 34:5; Zech. 10:2
Matt. 10:15	Sodom & Gomorrah
Matt. 10:21	Family turn against each other – Micah 7:6
Matt. 10:25	The false god Beelzebub – 1Kings 1:2-3
Matt. 10:35-36	Enemies to be of your own household – Micah 7:6
Matt. 11:3	The Coming One – Deut. 18:15; Mal. 3:1
Matt. 11:5	Quote from Isa. 35:5-6; 61:1
Matt. 11:10	Quote of Mal. 3:1
Matt. 11:13	Law & Prophets
Matt. 11:14	Elijah who was to come – Mal. 4:5
Matt. 11:21-22	Tyre & Sidon – Ezek. 26:3, 4, 15-21
Matt. 11:23-24	Sodom – Gen. 19:24, 28

Matt. 11:29	Rest for your souls – Jer. 6:16
Matt. 12:3-4	David-consecrated bread – 1Sam. 21:6
Matt. 12:5	Priests break Law on the Sabbath
Matt. 12:7	Quote Hosea 6:6
Matt. 12:8	Lord of the Sabbath – Exodus 20:1, 8
Matt. 12:18-21	Quote Isaiah 42:1-4
Matt. 12:23	Son of David – Psalm 132:11
Matt. 12:39	The prophet Jonah – Jonah 1:1
Matt. 12:40	Jonah 1:17
Matt. 12:41	Nineveh, Jonah, greater than Jonah
Matt. 12:42	Queen of Sheba, greater Solomon – 1Kings 10:1-10
Matt. 13:9, 13	Eyes do not see, ears do not hear - Isa. 6:9; Jer. 5:21
Matt. 13:14-15	Quote Isaiah. 6:9-10
Matt. 13:32	Quote Ezekiel 17:23; Daniel 4:12
Matt. 13:35	Quote Psalm 78:2
Matt. 13:41	Reference to Zephaniah 1:2-3 note
Matt. 13:43	Quote Daniel 12:3
Matt. 15:4	Quote Ex. 20:12, 17; Lev. 20:9; Deut. 5:16
Matt. 15:7-9	Quote Isaiah 29:13
Matt. 15:13	God's planting – Isaiah 60:21; 61:3
Matt. 15:22	Canaanite, O' Son of David – Psa. 132:11
Matt. 16:4	The sign of Jonah – Jonah 1:17
Matt. 16:13	Daniel 7:13
Matt. 16:14	Elijah, Jeremiah, one of the prophets
Matt. 16:16	Christ (Messiah) – Daniel 9:26
Matt. 16:21	Christ alive – Dan. 9:26; Psa. 16:10-11; Isa. 53:10-12

Matt. 16:27	According to one's deeds – Psa. 62:12; Prov. 24:12
Matt. 17:3-4	Moses and Elijah
Matt. 17:9,12	Son of Man, rise from dead – Dan. 9:26; Psa. 16:10-11
Matt. 17:10-13	Elijah/John the Baptist – Malachi 3:5
Matt. 17:22-23	Son of Man, killed, & alive – Dan. 9:26; Psa. 16:10
Matt. 18:16	Requires 2-3 witnesses – Deut. 17:6, 19:15
Matt. 19:4-5	Created male & female – Gen. 1:27, 2:24; 5:2
Matt. 19:7	Moses & Divorce – Deut. 24:1
Matt. 19:17	The Commandments -- B Lev. 18:5; Ezekiel 20:11
Matt 19:18-19	Specific commandments – Ex. 20:12-16; Lev. 19:18
Matt. 19:28	Messiah's throne/12 tribes – Psa. 45:6, 93:2
Matt. 20:28	A ransom for many – Isaiah 53:4-6, 8-12
Matt. 20:30-31	Son of David – 2Kings 8:19; Psalm 89:35-36
Matt. 21:4-5	Quote Zechariah 9:9
Matt. 21:9	Quote Psalm 118:26
Matt. 21:13	Quote Isaiah 56:7; Jeremiah 7:11
Matt. 21:16	Quote Psalm 8:2
Matt. 21:33	Israel as God's vineyard – Isiah 5:1-2, 7
Matt. 21:42	Quote Psalm 118:22-23
Matt. 22:24	Marrying a dead brother's wife – Deut. 25:5
Matt. 22:32	Quote Exodus 3:6
Matt. 22:37	Quote Deuteronomy 6:5
Matt. 22:39	Quote Leviticus 19:18

Matt. 22:42-45	Son of David, Lord – 2Sam. 23:2; Psa. 110:1
Matt. 23:5	Phylacteries – Exodus 13:16
Matt. 23:23	Reference to Micah 6:8
Matt. 23:34	Treatment of the prophets – 2Chron. 36:15-16
Matt. 23:35	Murder Abel to Zachariah – Gen. 4:8; Zech. 1:1
Matt. 23:39	Quote Psalm 18:26
Matt. 24:5,11	False prophets – Jer. 29:8-9
Matt. 24:15	Abomination of desolation – Dan. 9:27; 11:31; 12:11
Matt. 24:21	The great tribulation – Daniel 12:1; Joel 2:2
Matt. 24:29	Isa. 13:10; Ezek. 32:7; Joel 2:10, 31
Matt. 24:30	Son of Man with the clouds – Dan. 7:13; Zech. 12:10
Matt. 24:31	Isa. 27:13; Zech. 9:14
Matt. 24:37-39	Noah entered the ark & flood – Gen. 7:7, 11
Matt. 25:32	Shepherd separates sheep from goats – Ezek. 37:17, 20
Matt. 25:35-36	Met other's needs -- Isa. 58:7; Ex. 18:7
Matt. 26:2-5	Passover/kill Christ – Psa. 22:16; Dan. 9:26; Isa. 53:5
Matt. 26:15	30 pieces of silver -- Zech. 11:12
Matt. 26:17-19	Passover / Unleavened Bread – Ex. 12:17-18
Matt. 26:31	Quote Zech. 13:7
Matt. 26:54, 56	Jesus refers to the Scriptures (Old Testament)
Matt. 26:64	Jesus refers to Psalm 110:1; Dan. 7:13
Matt. 27:7-10	The Potter's field – Zech. 11:12; Jer. 32:25

Matt. 27:34	Quote Psalm 69:21
Matt. 27:35	Quote Psalm 22:18
Matt. 27:39, 43	Reference to Psa. 22:7-8; 109:25
Matt. 27:38, 44	Those crucified with Jesus -- Isa. 53:9
Matt. 27:46	Jesus quotes Psalm 22:1
Matt. 27:47, 49	Reference to the prophet Elijah
Matt. 27:51	Veil separating the Holy of Holies -- Ex. 26:31-33
Matt. 27:57-60	Reference to Isa. 53:9
Matt. 28:18	Jesus given all authority -- Daniel 7:13-14

Endnotes

[1] Kenneth C. Davis. <u>Don't Know Much About the Bible</u>. William Morrow and Company, Inc. 1998. p. 350.

[2] Ibid.

[3] John McRay. <u>Archaeology and the New Testament</u>. Baker Book House, 1991. p. 361. Referencing Aland and Aland Text of the New Testament.

[4] Ibid.

[5] C.S. Lewis. <u>Mere Christianity</u>. The Macmillan Company. 1952. p. 29.

[6] <rationalchristianity.net/only_way.html> "How Can Christians Say Jesus Is the Only Way To God."

[7] C.S. Lewis. <u>That Hideous Strength</u>. Collier Books, 1962. p. 72.

[8] Stanley Grenz. "The Universality of the 'Jesus Story'." James G. Stackhouse Jr. (ed). <u>No Other Gods Before Me?</u> Baker Academic, 2001. p. 107.

[9] Gerald Pillay. "No God's-Eye View." <u>No Other Gods Before Me?</u> p. 124.

[10] Ravi Zacharias. <u>Jesus Among Other Gods: The absolute Claims of the Christian Message</u>. Word Publishing, 2000. p. 7.

[11] Isaiah 45:5-21. There are many such statements including condemning other so-called gods as frauds. Exodus 20:3-5; Deuteronomy 4:15-39; 2Sam. 22:32; Isa. 41:20-24; 42:8; 46:5-10. John 14:6; Acts 4:12

[12] C.S. Lewis. <u>That Hideous Strength</u>. Collier Books, 1962.

[13] Josh McDowell and Don Stewart. <u>Answers to tough Questions Skeptics Ask About the Christian Faith</u>. Here's Life Publishers, 1980. pp. 145-146.

[14] Josh McDowell and Don Stewart. <u>Answers to tough Questions Skeptics Ask About the Christian Faith</u>. p. 148.

[15] John McRay. <u>Archaeology and the New Testament</u>. p. 20.

[16] Ibid, p. xxxii

[17] Jack P. Lewis. <u>Archaeological Backgrounds to Bible People</u>. Baker Book House, 1971. p. 177.

[18] Randall Price. <u>The Stones Cry Out</u>. p. 316.

[19] <josh.org/arcaeology-validates-Bible?utm_source=google&utm_medium=cpc&utm>

[20] Titus Kennedy. <u>Excavating the Evidence for Jesus</u>. pp. 19, 21.

[21] Titus Kennedy. <u>The Essential Archaeological Guide to Bible Lands</u>. p. 300.

[22] Thomas Paine. <u>The Age of Reason</u>. the Thomas Paine Foundation. Original publication 1794-1795. Reprint, N.D. pp. 11-12.

[23] Mark D. Roberts. "Are the birth Narratives Historical?" (section B). Mark D. Roberts.com

[24] Ibid.

25 Ibid.

26 Randall Price w/ H Wayne House. Zondervan Handbook of Biblical Archaeology. Zondervan Academic, 2017. pp. 237-239.

27 John McRay. Archaeology and the New Testament. Baker Book House, 1991. p. 91.

28 David E. Graves. The Archaeology of the New Testament. Electronic Christian Media, 2019. pp. 36-37. Referencing Mark Kidger. The Star of Bethlehem: An Astronomer's View. Princeton University Press, 1999. 46; James D. G. Dunn. Jesus Remembered. Eerdmans, 2003. 234. Jack Finigan, E. Jerry Varaman, & Edwin M. Yamauchi (eds) Chronos, Kairos, Christos Eisenbrauns, 1989. 97-117.

29 John McRay. Archaeology and the New Testament. p. 157.

30 Titus Kennedy. The Essential Archaeological Guide to Bible Lands. p. 300.

31 Titus Kennedy. Excavating the Evidence for Jesus. p. 24. Referencing Oxythynchus papyrus 255.

32 John McRay. Archaeology and the New Testament. p. 155. This decree is held in the British Museum, papyrus 904.

33 Titus Kennedy. Excavating the Evidence for Jesus. pp. 25-26.

34 John McRay. Archaeology and the New Testament. p. 154. Referencing G.H.R. Horsley. New Documents Illustrating Early Christianity. Macquarie University Press. Vol. 4. p. 182.

35 Jack P. Lewis. Archaeological Backgrounds to Bible People. p. 138.

36 Randall Price w/ H Wayne House. Zondervan Handbook of Biblical Archaeology. p. 235. referencing Kenneth Bailey. "The Manger and The Inn." Associates for Biblical Research, <www.bibleaercheology.org/post/ 2008/11/08/The-manger-and-the-Inn.aspx#Article> & E.F.F. Bishop. Jesus of Palestine. Lutterworth, 1955. p. 42.

37 John McRay. Archaeology and the New Testament. p.156. Referencing Justin Martyr. Dialogue With Trypho, 78. The 2nd century apocryphal Protevangelium of James includes the same information.

38 Titus Kennedy. Excavating the Evidence for Jesus. p. 32. Citing Justin Martyr. Dialogue With Trypho. Origin Contra Celsum and other writings.

39 Jack Finegan. The Archaeology of the New Testament. Princeton University Press, 1969. pp. 22-23.

40 Jack Finegan. The Archaeology of the New Testament. p. 35.

41 Titus Kennedy. Excavating the Evidence for Jesus. pp. 32-33. Origin in his Contra Celsus quoting from The True Word by Celsus.

[42] Titus Kennedy. <u>Excavating the Evidence for Jesus</u>. pp. 53-55. Herod, out of paranoia killed three of his own sons around the same time as the massacre of the children. The apocryphal gospel Kennedy refers to is the <u>Protoevangelium of James</u>. A Jewish writing thought to be of the first century, <u>The Assumption of Moses</u> appears to allude to the massacre. The unknown author compares Herod to the Pharaoh who ordered the execution of Hebrew male babies.

[43] Randall Price w/ H Wayne House. <u>Zondervan Handbook of Biblical Archaeology.</u> p. 241.

[44] Randall Price w/ H Wayne House. <u>Zondervan Handbook of Biblical Archaeology.</u> p. 264.

[45] John McRay. <u>Archaeology and the New Testament</u>. pp. 203-204. Referencing Antonio Frova. "L'Inscrizionenzio Pilat a Cesarea." Rendiconti 95 (1961): 419-34>

[46] Titus Kennedy. <u>Excavating the Evidence for Jesus</u>. pp. 86-87.

[47] <biblearchaeologyreport.com/2019/01/19/top-tendiscoveries-in-biblical-arcaheolgy-relating-to the new-testament>

[48] Titus Kennedy. <u>Excavating the Evidence for Jesus</u>. p. 121. Mishna *Kerithoth* 1.6-7, & *Megillah* 29.

[49] Titus Kennedy. <u>Excavating the Evidence for Jesus</u>. pp. 86-87.

[50] <biblearchaeologyreport.com/2019/01/19/top-tendiscoveries-in-biblical-arcaheolgy-relating-to the new-testament>

[51] Bryant G. Wood & Clifford A. Wilson. "Temple Stones Unearthed." <u>Bible and Spade</u> Vol. 1, No. 1 Winter, 1972. p. 14. Referencing Josephus <u>Wars of the Jews</u>, VII, 1:1 and <u>Jerusalem Post Weekly</u>, January 11, 1973 & August 3, 1971.

[52] Titus Kennedy. <u>Excavating the Evidence for Jesus</u>. p. 95. Josephus, <u>Antiquities</u> 18, 116-117.

[53] Ibid. p. 91. Referencing Josephus, <u>Antiquities</u> 18.237, 19.275, 20.138.

[54] Jack P. Lewis. <u>Archaeological Backgrounds to Bible People</u>. p. 148.

[55] Titus Kennedy. <u>Excavating the Evidence for Jesus</u>. pp. 91-92. Josephus, <u>Antiquities</u> 17.21-27.

[56] Jack P. Lewis. <u>Archaeological Backgrounds to Bible People</u>. p. 156. Referencing Josephus, <u>Antiquities</u> xvii 11.4 (317), 13.1, 2,4 (340-349 f.) <u>War</u> ii. 6.3 (93), 11. 7.3. 4 (111, 114) i. 32.7,33.7 (646, 664).

[57] Ibid. p. 92.

[58] Titus Kennedy. <u>Excavating the Evidence for Jesus</u>. pp. 214-215.

[59] Randall Price. <u>The Stones Cry Out</u>. p. 316.

[60] Titus Kennedy. <u>Excavating the Evidence for Jesus</u>. pp. 137- 139.

[61] Jack Finegan. The Archaeology of the New Testament. p, 146. Some later manuscripts have an interpolation that was someone's added attempt to explain the troubling of the water by an angel.

[62] Ibid, p. 139.

[63] Donald E. Demaray. Bible Study Source-Book. Zondervan Publishing House, 1964. p. 243.

[64] Ibid. pp. 108-109. Reference to Josephus. Wars. The boat can be viewed at Yigal Allon Center at Kubbutz Ginosar.

[65] John McRay. Archaeology and the New Testament. pp. 163-164.

[66] Titus Kennedy. Excavating the Evidence for Jesus. pp. 86-87.

[67] John McRay. Archaeology and the New Testament. pp. 164-165.

[68] Titus Kennedy. The Essential Archaeological Guide to Bible Lands. p. 291. Referencing Josephus, Life, 403-404; Josephus Wars, 3,519-521.

[69] Titus Kennedy. The Essential Archaeological Guide to Bible Lands. Harvest House Publishers, 2023. p. 292.

[70] Jack Finegan. The Archaeology of the New Testament. p. 51.

[71] Randall Price w/ H Wayne House. Zondervan Handbook of Biblical Archaeology. p. 249.

[72] Titus Kennedy. The Essential Archaeological Guide to Bible Lands. p. 297.

[73] Titus Kennedy. The Essential Archaeological Guide to Bible Lands. pp. 297-299.

[74] David E. Graves. The Archaeology of the New Testament. pp. 82-83. Referencing Josephus, Aniquities of the Jews, 18.119.

[75] Ibid.

[76] Titus Kennedy. The Essential Archaeological Guide to Bible Lands. p. 304-306. Referencing Josephus, Wars, 3,446-461.

[77] Titus Kennedy. Excavating the Evidence for Jesus. pp. 117-118.

[78] Randall Price w/ H Wayne House. Zondervan Handbook of Biblical Archaeology. p. 251. This includes a photo of 'the seat of Moses'

[79] Titus Kennedy. Excavating the Evidence for Jesus. p. 126. Referencing Josephus, Wars 2.232-238; Antiquities 13. 7479, 18.29-30.

[80] Jack Finegan. Light From the Ancient Past: The Archaeological Background of the Hebrew-Christian Religion. Princeton University Press, 1946. p. 232.

[81] Jack Finegan. Light From the Ancient Past: p. 232.

[82] Titus Kennedy. Excavating the Evidence for Jesus. pp. 125-127.

[83] Titus Kennedy. The Essential Archaeological Guide to Bible Lands. p. 255.

[84] <biblearchaeologyreport.com/2019/01/19/top-tendiscoveries-in-biblical-arcaheolgy-relating-to the new-testament>

[85] Randall Price. The Stones Cry Out. p. 317.

[86] Titus Kennedy. The Essential Archaeological Guide to Bible Lands. p. 288.

[87] Titus Kennedy. Excavating the Evidence for Jesus. p. 175.

[88] Titus Kennedy. The Essential Archaeological Guide to Bible Lands. p. 287.

[89] Titus Kennedy. Excavating the Evidence for Jesus. p. 197.

[90] Titus Kennedy. Excavating the Evidence for Jesus. p. 194.

[91] Titus Kennedy. Excavating the Evidence for Jesus. p. 195. Referencing Sanhedrin 43a; Sanhedrin 107b; Sotah 47a.

[92] Titus Kennedy. Excavating the Evidence for Jesus. p. 181.

[93] Titus Kennedy. Excavating the Evidence for Jesus. pp. 183-184.

[94] Titus Kennedy. Excavating the Evidence for Jesus. pp. 198-199.

[95] Jack Finegan. The Archaeology of the New Testament. p. 90.

[96] Jack Finegan. The Archaeology of the New Testament. pp. 91-92.

[97] Randall Price w/ H Wayne House. Zondervan Handbook of Biblical Archaeology. pp. 253-254.

[98] Randall Price w/ H Wayne House. Zondervan Handbook of Biblical Archaeology. pp. 253-255.

[99] Randall Price w/ H Wayne House. Zondervan Handbook of Biblical Archaeology. pp. 255-256.

[100] Titus Kennedy. Excavating the Evidence for Jesus. p. 200.

[101] Titus Kennedy. Excavating the Evidence for Jesus. p. 201.

[102] Ibid.

[103] Titus Kennedy. Excavating the Evidence for Jesus. pp. 202-203.

[104] Jack Finegan. Light From the Ancient Past: The Archaeological Background of the Hebrew-Christian Religion. p. 236.

[105] Titus Kennedy. Excavating the Evidence for Jesus. pp. 207-209.

[106] Josh McDowell and Don Stewart. Answers to tough Questions Skeptics Ask About the Christian Faith. Here's Life Publishers, 1980. pp. 82-83.

[107] Ibid.

[108] Titus Kennedy. Excavating the Evidence for Jesus. pp. 208-209.

[109] Titus Kennedy. The Essential Archaeological Guide to Bible Lands. p. 165. Referencing Talmud Shabbat 15a; Babylonian Talmud Sanhedrin 88b.

[110] Titus Kennedy. Excavating the Evidence for Jesus. p. 210.

[111] Titus Kennedy. Excavating the Evidence for Jesus. pp. 219-221.

[112] Titus Kennedy. Excavating the Evidence for Jesus. p. 216. Referencing Josephus Antiquities 18.2.

[113] Titus Kennedy. Excavating the Evidence for Jesus. pp. 217-218.

[114] Titus Kennedy. Excavating the Evidence for Jesus. p. 238. Referencing Philo of Alexandria, Embassy to Gaius. 299-305.

[115] Titus Kennedy. Excavating the Evidence for Jesus. pp. 218-219.

[116] Titus Kennedy. Excavating the Evidence for Jesus. p. 90.

[117] Titus Kennedy. Excavating the Evidence for Jesus. p. 222.

[118] Titus Kennedy. p. 223.

[119] Referencing Josephus. Antiquities. 20.197-203. Also, Titus Kennedy Excavating the Evidence for Jesus. p. 223.

[120] Titus Kennedy. Excavating the Evidence for Jesus. p. 228.

[121] Titus Kennedy. Excavating the Evidence for Jesus. p. 228.

[122] Titus Kennedy. Excavating the Evidence for Jesus. p. 229. Referencing Appian, Civil Wars & Josephus, Wars.

[123] Titus Kennedy. Excavating the Evidence for Jesus. p. 229. Josephus, Antiquities & Wars; Lucian, Piscator; Cicero, Verres.

[124] Titus Kennedy. Excavating the Evidence for Jesus. p. 229. Referencing Plutarch, Coriolanus; Platus, Miles Gloriosus & Carbonaria; Clodius, History; Melito of Sardis Passion; Artemidorus, Oneirokritikon.

[125] David E. Graves. The Archaeology of the New Testament. p. 97. Referencing Joel B. Green, Scot McKnight, and I. Howard Marshal (eds)., Dictionary of Jesus and the Gospels. Intervarsity Pres, 192. p. 150.

[126] Titus Kennedy. Excavating the Evidence for Jesus. pp. 239-240. Hadrian purposely obscured the location by constructing a temple there to Venus. The so-called Gordon's Calvary was chosen due to confusion of the meaning of the Aramaic word, and its slight resemblance to a skull's face is due to quarrying much later during the Ottoman era.

[127] Randall Price. The Stones Cry Out. p. 310.

[128] John McRay. Archaeology and the New Testament. p. 206. Referring to William Edwards et al., "On the Physical Death of Jesus Christ," Journal of the American Medical Association 255.11 (21 March 1986: 1461).

[129] Randall Price w/ H. Wayne House. Zondervan Handbook of Biblical Archaeology. pp. 258-259.

[130] Randall Price w/ H. Wayne House. Zondervan Handbook of Biblical Archaeology. p. 261.

[131] Randall Price. The Stones Cry Out. pp. 310-311.

[132] Randall Price. The Stones Cry Out. p. 311.

[133] Titus Kennedy. Excavating the Evidence for Jesus. pp. 230-231.

[134] Titus Kennedy. Excavating the Evidence for Jesus. p. 231.

135 <biblearchaeologyreport.com/2019/01/19/top-tendiscoveries-in-biblical-arcaheolgy-relating-to the new-testament>

136 Pseudepigraphal refers to writings that were falsely and deliberately attributed to well-known people. It was an attempt to obtain acceptance and trust in the reliability of the writing.

137 Titus Kennedy. Excavating the Evidence for Jesus. p. 167.

138 Titus Kennedy. Excavating the Evidence for Jesus. p. 167.

139 Titus Kennedy. Excavating the Evidence for Jesus. pp. 168-169. The inscription: "[unknown] son of Joseph" may have read "Hunan." The 'documentary' assumes this to be Jesus. The tomb held the bones of at least 35 people spanning probably four or five generations.

140 Titus Kennedy. Excavating the Evidence for Jesus. p. 169.

141 Ibid, pp. 169-170.

142 Titus Kennedy. Excavating the Evidence for Jesus. pp. 170-171.

143 Titus Kennedy. Excavating the Evidence for Jesus. p. 171.

144 John McRay. Archaeology and the New Testament. p. 206.

145 Jack Finegan. The Archaeology of the New Testament. pp. 137-138, 164. Referring to Eusebius' Life of Constantine III26 NPNFSSI, p. 527.

146 Jack Finegan. The Archaeology of the New Testament. p. 164.

147 John McRay. Archaeology and the New Testament. p. 157.

148 John McRay. Archaeology and the New Testament. pp. 213-214.

149 David E. Graves. The Archaeology of the New Testament. p. 87. Citing Norman Geisler and Joseph M. Holden. Popular Handbook of Archaeology and the Bible. Harvest House, 2013. p. 309.

150 David E. Graves. The Archaeology of the New Testament. p. 95.

151 David E. Graves. The Archaeology of the New Testament. pp. 94-95. Referencing Andrew Cockburn. "The Judas Gospel." National Geographic. 209, No. 9 (2006). pp. 78-95. Sandra Scham. "An Apology for Judas." Archaeology 59, No. 4 (2006), pp. 50-51. Craig Evans. Fabricating Jesus: How modern Scholars Distort the Gospels. IVP Books, 2006. pp. 240-241.

152 Darrell Bock. "The Good News of Da Vinci." Christianity Today. January 1, 2004. p. 62. <www.christianitytoday.com/ct/2004/january/2004/23.62.html>

153 Randall Price w/ H. Wayne House. Zondervan Handbook of Biblical Archaeology. Zondervan Academic, 2017. p. 233.

154 Ibid.

155 William M. Ramsey. St. Paul the Traveller and the Roman Citizen. Baker Book House. Reprint 1962. pp. 4, 10, 14.

156 Ibid, p. 14.

[157] William Whiston (Trans). Josephus Complete Works. "Antiquities." XX.5.1.

[158] John McRay. Archaeology and the New Testament. p. 139.

[159] Titus Kennedy. The Essential Archaeological Guide to Bible Lands. pp. 279-281. Referencing Josephus, Wars 7:23; Philo, Embassy, 305.

[160] Jack Finegan. The Archaeology of the New Testament. p. 70.

[161] Ibid, pp. 70-71.

[162] John McRay. Archaeology and the New Testament. pp. 140-142.

[163] John McRay. Archaeology and the New Testament. p. 227. Referencing Strabo, Geography 16.2.5; Josephus, Jewish Wars 7.3,3 (43).

[164] David E. Graves. The Archaeology of the New Testament. pp. 108-109.

[165] Titus Kennedy. The Essential Archaeological Guide to Bible Lands. p. 283. Referencing Josephus Antiquities 19. pp. 343-350.

[166] <biblearchaeologyreport.com/2019/01/19/top-tendiscoveries-in-biblical-arcaheolgy-relating-to the new-testament>

[167] Randall Price w/ H. Wayne House. Zondervan Handbook of Biblical Archaeology. p. 300.

[168] Titus Kennedy. The Essential Archaeological Guide to Bible Lands. p. 365. Referencing Josephus, Antiquities; Cicero, Pro Flacco.

[169] Titus Kennedy. The Essential Archaeological Guide to Bible Lands. p. 365. Referencing Pliny, Epistle 96; Martyrdom of Polycarp; Eusebius Ecclesiastical History; 1Peter 1:1, 6, 2:19-21, 3:14, 4:12-19; Revelation 2-3.

[170] Titus Kennedy. The Essential Archaeological Guide to Bible Lands. pp. 368-369. Referencing Ovid, Metamorphoses, book 8.

[171] Titus Kennedy. The Essential Archaeological Guide to Bible Lands. p. 369. Referencing Stephanus of Byzantium, Ethnica.

[172] John McRay. Archaeology and the New Testament. pp. 288-289.

[173] John McRay. Archaeology and the New Testament. p. 373.

[174] John McRay. Archaeology and the New Testament. p. 226. Referencing Suetonius, Lives of the Caesars"Claudius"25.;Jack Finigan. Handbook of Biblical Chronology. Princedon University Press, 1964. p. 319.

[175] David E. Graves. The Archaeology of the New Testament. p. 109. Suetonius, Claudius. 5.25.4

[176] Ibid, p. 109, note 36.

[177] Randall Price w/ H. Wayne House. Zondervan Handbook of Biblical Archaeology. p. 301.

[178] Ibid.

[179] <biblearchaeologyreport.com/2019/01/19/top-tendiscoveries-in-biblical-arcaheolgy-relating-to the new-testament>

180 John McRay. Archaeology and the New Testament. pp. 331-332.

181 Randall Price. The Stones Cry Out. p. 317.

182 <biblearchaeologyreport.com/2019/01/19/top-tendiscoveries-in-biblical-arcaheolgy-relating-to the new-testament>

183 John McRay. Archaeology and the New Testament. pp. 373-374.

184 Randall Price w/ H. Wayne House. Zondervan Handbook of Biblical Archaeology. p. 314.

185 David E. Graves. The Archaeology of the New Testament. p. 118. Referencing Michael Fieger. Im Schatten der Artemis: Glaube und Ungehorsam in Ephesus Lang, 1998. pp. 83-86.

186 Randall Price w/ H. Wayne House. Zondervan Handbook of Biblical Archaeology. p. 312.

187 John McRay. Archaeology and the New Testament. p. 259. Referencing Barbara Levick. "Two Inscriptions from Pisidian Antioch." Anatolian Studies 15 (1965); 58-59.

188 David E. Graves. The Archaeology of the New Testament. p. 119.

189 David E. Graves. The Archaeology of the New Testament. p. 119. Referencing James R. Edwards. "Archaeology Gives New Reality to Paul's Ephesus Riot." Biblical Archaeology Review. 42, No. 4 (August 2016). pp. 24-33.

190 Ibid, pp. 119-120.

191 Titus Kennedy. The Essential Archaeological Guide to Bible Lands. p. 319. Referencing Strabo, Geography.

192 John McRay. Archaeology and the New Testament. p. 255. referencing Strabo, Geography 14.1.42.

193 David E. Graves. The Archaeology of the New Testament. p. 120.

194 Titus Kennedy. The Essential Archaeological Guide to Bible Lands. p. 320. Referencing: Apollonius of Tyana, Letters; Dio Chrysostom, Supplementum Epigraphicum Graecum EG 28.863 & Pliny, Natural History.

195 John McRay. Archaeology and the New Testament. p. 247. Referencing William Ramsey, Cities and Bishoprics 1.72.

196 David E. Graves. The Archaeology of the New Testament. pp. 123-125. Referencing Adrian N. Sherwin-White. "The Roman Citizenship: A Survey of Its Development into a World Franchise." Hildegard Temporini & Wolfgang House (eds.) Aufstieg und Niedergang der romischen Welt; Geschichte und Kulter Rom sim Spiegal der neuren Forshung. De Gruyter, 1974. pp. 23-58. Henry Sanders. "The Birth Certificate of a Roman Citizen." Classical Philology. 22, No. 4 (1927); pp. 409-413. Peter Garnsey. Social Status and Legal Privilege in the Roman Empire. Oxford University Press, 1970.

[197] David E. Graves. <u>The Archaeology of the New Testament</u>. pp. 124-125.

[198] Jack P. Lewis. <u>Archaeological Backgrounds to Bible People</u>. pp. 150-152.

[199] Titus Kennedy. <u>The Essential Archaeological Guide to Bible Lands</u>. p. 161.

[200] Titus Kennedy. <u>The Essential Archaeological Guide to Bible Lands</u>. p. 263.

[201] David E. Graves. <u>The Archaeology pf the New Testament</u>. pp. 129-130. Referencing Sandra J. Bingham. "The Praetorian Guard in the Political and Social Life of Julio-Claudian Rome." (Ph.D. diss. The University of British Columbia, 1997). p. 39.

[202] John McRay. <u>Archaeology and the New Testament</u>. pp. 339-340.

[203] Randall Price. <u>The Stones Cry Out</u>. p. 316.

[204] David E. Graves. <u>The Archaeology of the New Testament</u>. p. 89.

[205] David E. Graves. <u>The Archaeology pf the New Testament</u>. p. 133. Referencing Yotam Tepper & Leah di Segni. "A Christian Prayer Hall of the third century." pp. 36-40, Figure 88.

[206] David E. Graves. <u>The Archaeology pf the New Testament</u>. p. 133.

[207] David E. Graves. <u>The Archaeology pf the New Testament.</u> p. 136. Referencing Tacitus, <u>Annuals</u>. 3.69.

[208] David E. Graves. <u>The Archaeology pf the New Testament</u>. pp. 136-137. Referencing Pliny <u>Natural History</u>, 4.13.69; Tacitus <u>Annuals</u>, 4.30.

[209] Titus Kennedy. <u>The Essential Archaeological Guide to Bible Lands</u>. pp. 326-327. Referencing Strabo, <u>Geography</u>; Cicero, <u>Pro Flacco</u>; Tacitus, <u>Annuals</u>

[210] Titus Kennedy. <u>The Essential Archaeological Guide to Bible Lands</u>. pp. 329-334. Referencing Pliny, <u>Natural History</u>; Josephus, <u>Antiquities</u>; Strabo, <u>Geography</u>; Tacitus, <u>Annals</u>; Irenaeus <u>Against Heresies</u>.

[211] Titus Kennedy. <u>The Essential Archaeological Guide to Bible Lands</u>. pp. 335-336, 402.

[212] David E. Graves. <u>The Archaeology pf the New Testament</u>. p. 188. Reference from Peter Wood. "Local Knowledge of the Letters of the Apocalypse." <u>Expository Times</u> 73 (1962 1961). pp. 163-164.

[213] David E. Graves. <u>The Archaeology pf the New Testament</u>. p. 189. Referencing David Gordon Mitten. "Anew Look at Ancient Sardis" <u>Biblical Archaeology</u>. 29, No. 3 (1966). pp. 38-68. Tacitus, <u>Annuals</u> 2.47; Pliny, Natural History. 2.86.200; Strabo, <u>Geography</u> 13.4.8.

[214] Titus Kennedy. <u>The Essential Archaeological Guide to Bible Lands</u>. pp. 337-338.

[215] David E. Graves. <u>The Archaeology pf the New Testament</u>. p. 190. Referencing Dio Chrysostom, <u>Rhodiaca, To the People of Rhodes</u>. Loeb Classical Library, 358: Xenophon, "Hellenica," <u>Hellenic Writings</u>. Loeb Classical Library, 88.

216 Bryant G. Wood & Clifford A. Wilson. "Diggings from Turkey: Unto the Church in Sardis." Bible and Spade Vol. 1, No. 1. pp. 23-25. Referencing The Biblical Archaeologist, Vol. XXIX, No. 2, May 1966; Bulletin of the American Schools of Oriental Research, No. 203, October 1971.

217 Titus Kennedy. The Essential Archaeological Guide to Bible Lands. pp. 339-341.

218 Titus Kennedy. The Essential Archaeological Guide to Bible Lands. pp. 344-345. Galen, On Anatomical Procedures; Celsus, De Medicina; Turtullian, On the Soul. David E. Graves. The Archaeology pf the New Testament. p. 203. Strabo. Geography 12.8.20.

219 Titus Kennedy. The Essential Archaeological Guide to Bible Lands. p. 346.

220 Ibid.

221 Ibid, pp. 348-350.

222 Titus Kennedy. The Essential Archaeological Guide to Bible Lands. p. 410.

223 Titus Kennedy. The Essential Archaeological Guide to Bible Lands. p. 410.

224 John McRay. Archaeology and the New Testament. p. 295.

225 Titus Kennedy. The Essential Archaeological Guide to Bible Lands. p. 410.

226 Titus Kennedy. The Essential Archaeological Guide to Bible Lands. p. 410.

227 John McRay. Archaeology and the New Testament. p. 304. Referencing Philostratus Life of Apollonius 6.3 (trans. F.C. Conybeare) Harvard University Press, 1912.

228 John McRay. Archaeology and the New Testament. p. 304. Referencing Pausanias Description of Greece 1.2.4 (trans. Peter Levi. Penguin, 1984.

229 John McRay. Archaeology and the New Testament. p. 304. referencing Aratus Phaenomena 5.

230 Merrill Unger. Unger's Bible Handbook. Moody Press, 1966. p. 588.

231 <www.ncregister.com/blog/archaeological-proofs-of-the-new-testament> Referencing Dialogues.Laert. Zeno, c 19.

232 Titus Kennedy. The Essential Archaeological Guide to Bible Lands. p. 461. Referencing ILS 1.2683; CIL 3.6687.

233 Titus Kennedy. The Essential Archaeological Guide to Bible Lands. p. 461. Referencing Pliny, Letters; Tacitus, Annals.

234 John McRay. Archaeology and the New Testament. p. 355.

235 Randall Price w/ H Wayne House. Zondervan Handbook of Biblical Archaeology. p. 293.

236 John McRay. Archaeology and the New Testament. pp. 356-357.

[237] Many of my writings have been presentations of arguments and evidence that give a rational basis for believing what I and many others claim about the biblical documents. See my list of books at the end of this book.

[238] Thomas Paine. The Age of Reason: Being an Investigation of True and Fabulous Theology. The Thomas Paine Foundation, n.d. p. 10.

[239] Josh McDowell and Don Stewart. Answers to tough Questions Skeptics Ask About the Christian Faith. pp. 9, 11.

[240] Ibid, p. 10.

[241] The Old Testament is translated from the Hebrew text, but our New Testament most often quotes from the Greek Text (LXX) or even paraphrases the O.T. passage or applies the reference to a new situation. This has frequently caused confusion when comparing the Old Testament reference to the New Testament, and in some cases gives the illusion of a contradiction or discrepancy between them.

[242] J.P. Moreland. "The Historicity of the New Testament." <www.bethinking.org/is-the-bible-reliable/the historicity-of-the-new-testament/>

[243] John Dominic Crossan. The Essential Jesus: What Jesus Really Taught. HarperCollins Publishers. p. 2.

[244] Ibid, pp. 9-10.

[245] Randall Price. The Stones Cry Out. p. 297.

[246] Titus Kennedy. Excavating the Evidence for Jesus. Harvest House Publishers, 2022. pp. 295-296.

[247] John A.T. Robinson. Redating the New Testament. Westminster Press, 1976. Robinson, a skeptical theologian, and former bishop, wrote that the absence of any reference to the actual destruction of Jerusalem by the Romans indicates the New Testament documents had to have been written prior to 70 A.D. His reason for this conclusion was that the end of ceremonial Judaism would have been a very strong argument that Christianity had now replaced Judaism as God's vehicle on the earth. It is inconceivable that no mention of those events and such arguments would not have been used had that destruction not occurred prior to these writings. Robinson also mentioned that most of his fellow liberal scholars were unwilling to embrace evidence that contradicted their prior assumptions.

[248] Philip Jenkins. Hidden Gospels: How the Search for Jesus Lost Its Way. Oxford University Press, 2001. p. 104.

[249] Ibid, p.103. Referencing Majella Franzmann. Jesus in the Nag Hammadi Writings. T. and T. Clark, 1996.

250 Ibid, p. 108.

251 Lee Strobel. The case for Christ. Harper Collins, 1998. p. 150 Referencing Ian Wilson. Jesus: The Evidence. p. 107. And an interview with psychologist Gary R. Collins. pp. 145-153.

252 Kenneth C. Davis. Don't Know Much About the Bible. p. 355.

253 For evidence revealing the Roman requirement of returning to one's ancestral home for a census see under the section on archaeology.

254 Kenneth C. Davis. Don't Know Much About the Bible. p. 356.

255 John Dominic Crossan. The Essential Jesus. p. 24.

256 Some of these texts are completely in regard to the Resurrection while others include a segment on the Resurrection. J.N.D. Anderson. Christianity: The Witness of History. The Tyndale Press, 1969; Paul Copan & Ron Tacelli. Jesus' Resurrection Fact or Figment? InterVarsity Press, 2000; William Lane Craig. Reasonable Faith, Crossway Books, Rev. 1994; Michael Green. Who Is This Jesus? Thomas Nelson Publishers, 1992; Simon Greenleaf. The Testimony of the Evangelists: The Gospels Examined by the Rules of Evidence. 1874. Kregel Publications reprint 1995; Gary R. Habermas & Michael R. Licona. The Case for the Resurrection of Jesus. Kregal Publications, 2004. Timothy Keller. The Reason for God. Riverhead Books, 2008. Josh McDowell & Sean McDowell. More Than A Carpenter, Tyndale House Publishers, 2009. John Warwick Montgomery. History and Christianity. Inter-Varsity Press, 1965. J.P. Moreland. Scaling the Secular City: A Defense of Christianity. Baker Book House, 1987. Lee Strobel. The Case For Christ. Zondervan Publishing House. 1998. Gerald C. Tilley. Is Jesus Christ Alive? California Biblical University Press, 2019.

257 See: 1Corinthians 2:7-14. Verse 14 in particular expresses why it is possible to read the Bible and not see nor comprehend what is written. Presuppositions, one's prior preconceived ideas and assumptions and/or unwillingness to embrace the truth prevents understanding.

258 Earlier in the passage (vs. 15 ff) Jesus warns about false prophets as well as in Matt. Chapter 24. We have had televangelists and others who have falsely claimed to do exactly what 7:22 states in order to gain a following and wealth for themselves.

259 Jesus fulfilled many prophecies of the Old Testament and promised that He will return. The prophesies that remain as yet unfulfilled relate to his return when he comes back as the ruler and judge of the earth. This is one of those prophesies that are yet future.

260 Glory – See: Matthew 24:30; John 1:14; 17:1-5.

[261] The New World Translation of the Jehovah's Witnesses is completely unreliable having been made in an attempt to justify the prior heresies of the cult. The New American Bible and the Jerusalem Bible both mistranslates passages in order to justify some Roman Catholic doctrines such as works being part of attaining salvation.

[262] Randall Price. The Stones Cry Out. Harvest House Publishers, 1997. p. 316.

[263] American Humanist Association. July 5, 2004. U.S.A. Today. 01/30/2006.

[264] Paul Johnson. Jesus. Penguin Books, 2010. p. 4.

[265] Titus Kennedy. Excavating the Evidence for Jesus. p. 9.

[266] Josh McDowell. The New Evidence That Demands A Verdict. p. 122.

[267] Jack P. Lewis. Archaeological Backgrounds to Bible People. p. 141. Citing Josephus. Antiquities 20, 9,1 (200).

[268] Titus Kennedy. Excavating the Evidence for Jesus. pp. 216-217. Referencing Josephus. Antiquities. 20, 9.

[269] Paul L. Maier. "The Empty Tomb as History." Christianity Today. Vol. XIX, No. 13. March 28, 1975. pp. 4-6.

[270] F.F. Bruce. The New Testament Documents: Are They Reliable? Inter-Varsity Fellowship, 5th edition, 1960. p. 117.

[271] Josh McDowell. The New Evidence That Demands A Verdict. pp. 120-121.

[272] Ibid. p. 122.

[273] Jack P. Lewis. Archaeological Backgrounds to Bible People. p. 145. Citing Suetonius Claudius 25, 4.

[274] Josh McDowell. The New Evidence That Demands A Verdict. pp. 121-122.

[275] Ralph O. Muncaster. How Do We Know Jesus Is God? Harvest House Publishers, 2000. p. 13. Josh McDowell. The New Evidence That Demands A Verdict. p. 123.

[276] Lucian. The Passing of Peregrinus (11-13). Cited by Josh McDowell. The New Evidence That Demands A Verdict. p. 121. and <Brittanica.com/biography/Lucian>

[277] F.F. Bruce. The New Testament Documents: Are They Reliable? p. 114. Bruce gives more details in regard to the various Gentile sources.

[278] <www.britannica.com/biography/Galen>

[279] Titus Kennedy. Excavating the Evidence for Jesus. p. 294. Referencing Galen. De Differentiis Pulsuum. 3.3. c. 180 AD.

[280] Ralph O. Muncaster. How Do We Know Jesus Is God? p. 13.

[281] Titus Kennedy. Excavating the Evidence for Jesus. pp. 213-214. Justin Martyr. Dialogue With Trypho.

[282] F.F. Bruce. The New Testament Documents: Are They Reliable? p. 119.

[283] Ralph O. Muncaster. How Do We Know Jesus Is God? p. 12.

[284] Ibid, p. 6.

[285] Josh McDowell. The New Evidence That Demands A Verdict. Condensed and edited from chapter 8. pp. 168-192. There are many more fulfilled prophecies he lists that I have not included.

[286] The LXX is the abbreviation for the Septuagint, the translation of the Hebrew Scriptures into Greek, made prior to 200 B.C. This translation by Jewish Rabbi's uses the specific Greek word Parthenos for "Virgin" in Isaiah 7:14.

[287] Norman Geisler. "The Uniqueness of Jesus Christ." <www.bethinking.org>

[288] Robert Brow. Religion: Origins and Ideas. Tyndale Press, 1966. p. 92.

[289] Millard J. Erickson. Christian Theology. Baker Book House, 1985. p. 266. "When we speak of the incomprehensibility of God … we mean that we do not know his qualities or his nature completely and exhaustively. We know God only as he has revealed himself. While his self-revelation is doubtless consistent with his full nature and accurate, it is not exhaustive revelation. Further, we do not totally understand or know comprehensively that which he has revealed to us of himself."

Other Books by Dr. Gerald Charles Tilley

The Origin of Religion. The secular explanations as to the Origin of religion are rejected as lacking evidence and contradicting the evidence available.

The Uniqueness of the Christian Faith. (4th Edition). Professor Tilley explains more than a dozen ways historic, biblical Christianity is unique and does not fit in the same category as the world religions.

The Absurdity of Atheism. (2nd Edition). This book shows that science, history, and human reason prove atheism to be absurd. Some of the irrational and dishonest methods and attempts to justify atheism are exposed.

The Origin of the Mormon Religion. The historical background of the early 1800's, the lives of Joseph Smith and his family as well as the early history of the religion itself prove Mormonism (the LDS Church) to be anti-Christian. This refutes current claims to be a Christian Church.

The Two Faces of Islam. In most of the world, Islam is known as a violent religion that persecutes and kills opponents. In the West, Muslim advocates claim Islam is a religion of peace and reconciliation. The Quran presents both versions of Islam. One of these predominates throughout its history.

Defending the Christian Faith. (2nd Edition). This book consists of about a dozen apologetics essays that seek to show the authenticity, historicity, and reliability of the biblical scriptures and that the Christian Faith is true.

Colossians: The Supremacy & Sufficiency of Christ. This is a basic Greek word study and commentary on the Apostle Paul's letter to the Colossian Church.

Is Jesus Christ Alive? This brand-new book presents evidence including evidence outside of the Bible that Jesus rose from the dead. It also refutes theories devised to avoid the evidence and conclusion of the resurrection.

The Protestant Reformations of the 16th Century. This book presents many of the participants in the Lutheran, Calvinist, and Anabaptist Reformations.

Made in the USA
Columbia, SC
10 November 2024

45934924R00089